Bruges

ges

···e fifteenth century that led to the triumph of
···y first. The silting up of its outlet to the sea brought to an
··· Bruges as Europe's leading centre of trade – everything trans-
···most overnight, to Antwerp. Citizens abandoned their splendid art
···city and most of those who stayed fell into abject poverty.
···ly nothing was built for almost four centuries, and relatively little of
··· was demolished. For these reasons, with the exception of Venice, no
···pean city has survived that can be so completely identified with the
···es. Other Belgian cities have splendid market squares and cathedrals
··· of them is it possible to observe such a completely medieval scene.
···sy to follow itineraries are suggested in this book all beginning at the
··· taking in the important locations without doubling back. There is
···to spend in churches and art galleries, or at serious beer-tasting ses-
···search purposes only, of course). One can undoubtedly spend at least
··· this gothic gem of a city without exhausting all that it has to offer.

Ghent

···s link Bruges with Ghent in less than half an hour, perhaps the main
···y Ghent is the most popular choice for a day excursion. However, as
···s more listed buildings than anywhere else in Belgium, plus the coun-
···t outgoing people, who enjoy an exuberant nightlife, it seems a pity
···d at least one night in the city. Certainly not to be missed is the Van
···Adoration of the Lamb of God' altarpiece in the cathedral, generally
···garded as the finest example of fifteenth century Flemish art.
···eshingly, Ghent has curbed excessive tourist despoliation, an advantage
···lly reserved for only the largest of the world's great cities. Most people
···streets are Ghent citizens going about their business, thereby establishing
a 'real' as opposed to an 'unreal' ambience. In both Bruges and Ghent, as elsewhere in Belgium, it is difficult to find anyone unable to speak English.

'I shall never run away to Bruges again without a copy of Christopher Turner's guide [to Bruges] (and a large box of hankies)'

Stephen Fry

Hotels/restaurants & Top Twelve Sights

Four Star Hotels ★ ★ ★ ★
- **A10** Best Western Navarra
- **A2** Brughe (ter)
- **A3** Bryghia
- **A10** Crowne Plaza
- **A38** Orangerie (De)
- **A4** Relais Oud Huis Amsterdam

Three Star Hotels ★ ★ ★
- **A5** Adornes
- **A24** Duc de Bourgogne
- **A37** Grand Hotel Oude Burg
- **A47** Ibis Brugge Centrum

Two Star Hotels ★ ★
- **A16** Cordoeanier
- **A1** Europ
- **A11** Imperial
- **A40** Lucca
- **A36** Salvators
- **A16** Voermanshuys ('t)

One Star Hotels ★
- **A28** Koffieboontje ('t)
- **A29** Putje ('t)

'H' Grade
- **A15** Central/Sirène d'Or
- **A18** Patritius

Guest Houses
- **A9** Mrs Deloof
- **A17** Mr & Mrs Gheeraert
- **A8** Mrs Nyssen
- **A21** Mrs de Vriese

Restaurants over 100 EUR
- **R24** Duc de Bourgogne
- **R19** Kapittel ('t)
- **R20** Karmeliet (De)
- **R33** Patrick Devos De Zilveren Pauw
- **R43** Snippe (De)
- **R22** Swaene (De)

Restaurants 75-100 EUR
- **R34** Bhavani
- **R39** Braamberg (Den)
- **R48** Kasteel Minnewater
- **R41** Lotteburg
- **R6** Paspartout (De)
- **R7** Spinola
- **R44** Tanuki
- **R23** Visscherie (De)

Restaurants 50-75 EUR
- **R45** Begijntje ('t)
- **R32** Belle Epoque
- **R15** Central

(unnamed)
- **R35** Celebrations Entertainment
- **R46** Maximiliaan van Oostenrijk
- **R26** Oud Brugge
- **R14** Sint-Joris

Restaurants below 75 EUR
- **R25** Breidel – De Coninck
- **R31** China
- **R27** Due Venezie (Le)
- **R42** Michelangelo
- **R13** Raadskelder
- **R12** Voske Malpertuus ('t)

Top Twelve Sights in Bruges
- **60** Augustijnenrei
- **49** Begijnhof
- **59** Belfry
- **53** 't Brugs Beertje
- **54** Groeninge Museum
- **58** Heilig Bloed Basiliek (Holy Blood Basilica)
- **50** Onze-Lieve-Vrouwekerk (Church of Our Lady)
- **56** Provinciaal Museum Het Brugse Vrije
- **55** Rozenhoedkaai
- **51** Sint Janshospitaal and Memling Museum
- **52** Sint Salvatorskathedraal (Cathedral of our Saviour)
- **57** Stadhuis (Town Hall)

Bruges

Contents

Welcome to
Bruges & Ghent

Top Twelve sights in Bruges

It is an invidious task to select some 'not-to-be-missed' locations from the wealth of delights that Bruges has to offer. The following selection is for visitors who have only a short time in the city.

Route 1

Belfry

The symbol of Bruges, this great bell tower, dating from 1282 overlooks Markt, the city's most important square. Its 366 steps to the octagonal lantern, at the top, may be climbed.

Groeninge Museum

Within a modern building are displayed the world's finest collection of Flemish Primitive paintings, many of them over 500 years old. The serenity of Van Eyck and the terrors of Hieronymus Bosch compete for attention.

Onze-Lieve-Vrouwekerk (Church of Our Lady)

Dating from the 13th century, this church, with a steeple that is the second highest brick structure in the world, is of greater interest than the cathedral nearby. Within can be admired Michelangelo's tender Virgin and Child sculpture, the15th century arms of England's King Edward IV, and the gilded tombs of Charles the Bold and Mary of Burgundy.

Begijnhof

Founded in 1245, the peaceful Begijnhof was laid out around a green as separate dwellings for impecunious single ladies who were prepared to live a semi-monastic existence. The Begijnhof church and a house fitted as a museum may be visited. Horse-drawn carriages end their route here.

Sint Janshospitaal and Memling Museum

Dating from the 13th century, this hospital is one of Europe's most ancient. Its old pharmacy and former chapel survive, the latter displaying six works painted by Hans Memling, including his famous Shrine of St Ursula.

Continued over page

Top Twelve sights in Bruges

(Route 1 Continued)

Heilig Bloed Basiliek (Holy Blood Basilica)

Located in a corner of Burg, the second most important square in Bruges, this, the oldest building to have survived in the city, comprises two oratory chapels, 12th century Romanesque on the ground floor and 15th century Gothic above. A tabernacle containing what is said to be Christ's blood is displayed on Fridays; its processional gold reliquary is kept in the museum.

Stadhuis (Town Hall)

Dominating Burg, the white sandstone Town Hall was completed in 1420, although its carved figures have been replaced twice.

Provinciaal Museum Het Brugse Vrije

Also located in Burg, the museum's great chimneypiece in the Aldermens' Room is its star attraction. One of the world's most exuberant, it was carved in 1529 to commemorate the Flemish repudiation of French suzerainty. Gothic and Renaissance features are incorporated in its design.

Route 2

Rozenhoedkaai

A staging point for boat trips on the canals, Rozenhoedkaai provides the most famous viewpoint in Bruges – looking over the picturesque little square of Huidenvettersplein towards the Belfry.

Route 3

Augustijnenrei

Approached from Vlamingstraat via an ancient stone bridge, Augustijnenrei (rei = canal) is considered by many to be the most tranquil stretch of the city's canals.

Route 4

Sint Salvatorskathedraal (Cathedral of our Saviour)

Basically medieval, the cathedral of Bruges has a splendid Gothic interior. Outstanding are the misericords of the stalls carved to honour the Order of the Golden Fleece, and a powerful depiction of God by master-carver Artus Quellin.

't Brugs Beertje

Located near Bruges cathedral, this tavern is regarded as the 'Cathedral of Belgian beer', more than 300 varieties being kept in stock.

History

Towards the end of the Roman Empire, Gallia Belgica, a province incorporating the Netherlands, was invaded from the north by a Germanic army; this proved unable to penetrate the great forest that then existed between the Rhine and the North Sea, and a frontier was established. Thus was created the Germanic north of Belgium and the Romanised south, a divide which is still manifest, primarily by language difference: the north of Belgium, including Bruges, speaking Dutch and the south speaking French. Only a vestige of the great forest has survived; it is known as the Zonienwoud and lies to the south of Brussels.

Following the break up of Charlemagne's Empire in 843, Flanders, an area that included what are now the provinces of East and West Flanders (Belgium), Zeeland (Holland) and Nord (France), fell under the control of Burgundian counts that were the vassals of the French kings. Boudewijn 'of the Iron Arm', the first Count of Flanders, built a fort in 862 to protect Bruges from Norse raiders, thus establishing the city. By tradition, the first living creature that Boudewijn saw in the region was a bear, which is why the city's coat of arms incorporates this animal. The name of Bruges may have derived from *brug* (bridge), although an alternative, *bruggia*, the Norse word for landing place, is equally possible. In the eleventh century the Counts of Flanders gradually extended their territory east of the River Schelde, acquiring what had been German possessions. Bruges was made the capital of Flanders in 1089, but it was 40 years before the first canal/rampart defences encircling the city were begun.

A great storm, known as the Dunkirk Flood, created the Zwin estuary in 1134; the River Reie flowed into it from Bruges, and virtually overnight the city became a navigable port with direct access to the North Sea.

It seems likely that the Romans introduced sheep to the region, and Flemish weavers became supreme clothmakers. Initially, local wool was used, but it soon became apparent that wool from England with its longer, silky fibres, produced a better quality cloth. Trade with England became all important to Bruges, and eventually the city obtained a monopoly on English wool – in 1282 it was established that only cloth made from English wool could be designated 'first class'. Unfortunately for Flanders, England and France had become deadly enemies, but although the Flemish were obliged to give tacit support to the King of France to whom they owed allegiance, they maintained commercial ties with England. In order to safeguard the English wool trade, Edward I invaded, occupying much Flemish territory; however, he soon had to return home to 'hammer' the Scots once more, and Philip the Fair, King of France, immediately reclaimed the land that Edward had captured. Philip constructed the second defensive 'envelopment' of Bruges in 1297, creating a double ring of canals and ramparts around the city.

Defeat of the French

In 1302, the Flemish trading guilds decided to put an end to French interference, and their members fought successfully against the trained soldiers of France, defeating them in the streets of Bruges ('the Matins of Bruges') and at the Battle of the Golden Spurs. Two years later, the French were defeated for a third time at the Battle of the Pevelenberg. Flanders had won a measure of independence, and trade prospered, partly due to its strategic location between the Mediterranean and Scandinavia. Eventually, around twenty mercantile nations were represented in Bruges, all with their own trading houses, and some with their own weighhouses.

In 1384, Flanders ceased to exist as a defined region due to its incorporation into the Burgundian dukedom following the death of the heirless Count of Flanders, Louis de Male. His daughter, Margaret, had married the Duke of Burgundy, Philip the Bold, in 1369, and he therefore added Flanders to his exisiting territories. Although the Burgundians spoke no Dutch, their period of rule, which lasted for less than a century, marked the golden age of Flanders.

Philip the Good

However it was Philip the Good (1396–1467) who was primarily responsible for the pre-eminence of the city; he became Duke in 1419, aged 23, transferring his capital from Dijon to Bruges. Philip greatly expanded his dukedom, either by force or by purchase, until, in 1443, the Burgundian Netherlands had acquired the dimensions of present day Belgium, Holland and Luxembourg combined.

In spite of his sybaritic fondness of luxury and art, Philip was an opportunist, bent on extending his power. Together with Henry V of England, he signed the Treaty of Troyes in 1420 by which England and Burgundy were ceded large areas of France. Subsequently, Philip befriended Edward IV during the late stages of the Wars of the Roses, sheltering him in Bruges and supporting his return to the English throne. Politically, however, Philip wished to remain on good terms with Charles, King of France, and refused to give Edward effective military support against him. Eventually, Philip even attempted to acquire Calais from England for his dukedom.

Charles the Bold inherited the dukedom from his father in 1467. He married Margaret of York, Edward IV's sister, and maintained the friendship between Burgundy and England. Unlike his father, however, he did not court good relations with France, battling continuously with Louis XI. In a complete reversal, Edward IV subsequently formed an alliance with the French King, fighting against whom Charles was killed at Nancy in 1477. As he left no male heir, the dukedom of Burgundy effectively came to an end. His daughter Mary, who only survived her father by five years, married Maximilian of Austria, and the long Habsburg rule of Bruges began in 1482.

Decline under the Habsburgs

Maximilian's tax measures against the citizens of Bruges led them to revolt in 1488, and they imprisoned him for 22 days. This political unrest, combined with the silting up of the Zwin estuary, presaged the downfall of Bruges, and merchants soon left for Antwerp.

Persecution of Protestants by the

In the 16th century, 53 Wollestraat, above, briefly housed the Holy Blood Relic

bigoted Spanish Habsburg rulers Charles V and his son Philip II led to further strife, in which the northern Netherlands broke away to form an independent Protestant state (Holland), whilst the southern Netherlands remained Catholic under Habsburg rule. The frontier, established by the Treaty of Munster in 1648, was arbitrarily delineated where the military activity had ended, and it has remained unaltered to this day.

The fortifications of Bruges were strengthened in 1614, bastion towers being erected for the first time. Ten years later, a canal link with Ghent was established. Nevertheless, the seventeenth century saw Bruges in decline, virtually all its trade having been transferred to Antwerp. It is surprising that Charles II, the exiled King of England, should have spent three years in the city (1656–59), an indication, perhaps, that some vestige of prosperity in Bruges remained.

Throughout the eighteenth century,

The Provincaal Hof, Markt

the southern Netherlands was given scant regard by its distant Habsburg rulers, whether from Madrid or, after 1713, from Vienna. In 1786, an English visitor to Bruges reported that there were so few inhabitants to be seen that the city looked as though it had been depopulated by the plague.

Bruges was occupied by Napoleon's army in 1795, full of anti-religious revolutionary zeal. Churches and monasteries were stripped of their treasures, most of which were sent to Paris from where, for almost 20 years, Bruges would be ruled. After Napoleon's defeat at Waterloo (south of Brussels) in 1815, the north and south Netherlands were reunited under the Treaty of Vienna. Sadly, in spite of good intentions, 236 years of separation had increased the differences between them to such a degree that amicable reunification proved impossible. The south Netherlanders rebelled in 1830 and a separate state – Belgium – was created, Prince Leopold of Saxe-Coburg, a favourite uncle of the future Queen Victoria, being invited to rule. Surprisingly, Bruges was made capital of West Flanders province, even though around half its inhabitants were by then in dire poverty.

Tourism begins

Help, however, was not far distant, its provider coming from an unexpected quarter, Bruges's old trading partner, England. Sentimentally visiting the Waterloo battlefield, many English had passed through Bruges and been struck by its antiquity. In 1820, the poet William Wordsworth recorded there 'a deeper peace than is in deserts found'. His sister Dorothy wrote 'its

inhabitants are accordant with the stateliness of former ages'. During the late-Victorian era, the British acquired a deep love of all things medieval, a love that was expressed in their art, literature and architecture – The Gothic Revival was very much in vogue.

Very soon, news about the romantic antiquity of Bruges spread in Great Britain, and a colony of British expatriates settled in the city, encouraging local architects to restore, or even to build anew, in Gothic Revival style. As a country, Belgium had become prosperous under Leopold II, even founding – rather late in the day – its own empire, the Belgian Congo. The port of Zeebrugge was built between 1895 and 1907, linked to Bruges by a canal, and Bruges once more had a maritime capability, albeit a limited one. The city expanded well outside its ramparts, and a railway station was built.

In 1892, Georges Rodenbach wrote *Bruges-la-Morte* (*Bruges the Dead*), and visitors flooded from the ports of Ostend and Blankenberghe to see this unique north European example of a petrified medieval city. Gradually throughout the twentieth century, tourism increased until it became by far the most important industry in Bruges. Fortunately, the romantic British immigrants had already impressed on Brugeans the importance of conservation, and strict town-planning controls were introduced at an early stage.

Bruges today

Although occupied by Germany during both World Wars, like Ghent, Bruges fortunately escaped physical damage, and its almost completely ancient appearance was undisturbed. Jealous accusations that the city has become an insipid 'theme park' do not really bear examination. Some buildings may have been somewhat over-restored or prettified excessively, but most examples of this are the result of nineteenth century over-enthusiasm. Moreover, it should be remembered that Bruges in its heyday was a city of crisp brickwork and fresh paint – as it is now – and those that would prefer to see it otherwise must surely be suffering from an excessive 'pleasure of ruins' romanticism. Conversely, most will find that the real upsetters in Bruges are the few modern buildings that have been permitted – particularly the hotel and municipal office block in Burg, on the site of the old cathedral, and the hotel in Oude Burg, behind Halle.

In spite of its inundation by tourists in the city centre, Bruges is an extremely popular place in which to live. Crowds of Brugeans descend on any centrally-located house that comes on the market, and peer through the windows as if a particularly gruesome murder had recently been committed within. This is because Brussels can be reached within the hour, and Eurocrats, including many from Britain, prefer to live away from the capital. Bruges is far from being a lifeless museum city.

The Flemish, their religion and their language

The great majority of Brugeans come from Flemish stock with Germanic origins, as do 60 per cent of all Belgians.

They tend to be serious-minded, but don't allow the work ethic to interfere too much with their leisure pursuits. All school-children in Belgium have Wednesday afternoons free, and a tradition has evolved that doting fathers, whenever possible, also take Wednesday afternoons off work to spend with them.

It might be noticed that two physical types prevail: one short, round-faced and chubby providing a startling contrast with the other, tall, thin and lantern-jawed (as depicted by Van Gogh in some of his early portraits of mining families). Most are Catholic, but the faith seems to be on the wane if Mass attendances are anything to go by. However, religious-inspired festivals (particularly if a holiday is involved) are supported enthusiastically.

Almost everyone speaks English well and is highly literate. Anti-Brussels diatribes from certain British politicians are offset by memories of the care and humanity shown by Belgian people after the *Herald of Free Enterprise* ferry sunk at Zeebrugge in 1987. British visitors are treated with particular affection; gratitude for the assistance given to Belgium in both World Wars and the consequent friendships made, seem to be passed down through the generations. It is also the British that still provide the majority of visitors who stay overnight in Bruges.

Local language

The official name of the language spoken in Bruges is Dutch (not Flemish). Apparently, Flemish Dutch is a rather antique version of the language, but there are no communication

Belgian chocolates

Ice sculptures from the Ice Festival in Bruges

the French version, Bruges, has been adopted by English-speaking people. Yet we manage to call its modern port, correctly, Zeebrugge, not Zeebruges – how convoluted is etymology!

Tourism is, of course, by far the most important industry in Bruges, and one would expect the residents to become a little tetchy with the hordes of camera-clicking visitors who never seem to know where they are, or where

difficulties between Dutch-speaking Belgians and Dutch-speaking Dutch. Surprisingly, however it is sometimes impossible for a citizen of Bruges to understand a citizen of Ghent, the nearest large town, who speaks in the local dialect. The word Dutch evolved in the Middle Ages from Dietse or Duutse, meaning 'the language of the people'. Deutsch (German) has the same source. Visitors will note that locally the city is called Brugge, but for some reason

Belgian waffles

Belgian beer

If conversation with a Belgian ever starts to flag, just raise the subject of beer. Eyes will sparkle, lips smack, and encyclopaedic knowledge will be imparted. More than 300 beers are produced in the country – a delight for the epicure. Just about every taste seems to be catered for; from weak to strong, light to heavy, sour to sweet – those who prefer a nice cup of tea can even have a tea-flavoured beer.

In general, the more esoteric the beer the higher the price will be, and those who wish to experiment should not plan on a cheap pub crawl. Several books have been written on the wonders of Belgian beer, which is a very complex subject. Not all visitors, it must be admitted, will like the rather egregious flavours of some varieties, particularly the sour, fruit-flavoured lambics and the highly alcoholic, rather sweet tripels. It is best to explain to the barman the type of flavour preferred and leave it to him.

Perhaps everyone should at least once try a raspberry-flavoured lambic, a trappist – on draft if possible – a tripel (very sweet) and a duvel (on the strong side). Wheat beer, eg Hoegaarden, is now becoming popular in England for its softness; it is much cheaper in Belgium! Those who are happy with a frothy, continental lager should just ask for a Pils, it will be very good, and much cheaper. However, whilst in Bruges it would be a pity not to drink the once locally-brewed Staffe Hendrik. It is of medium strength and usually served in special, elegant glasses – which may be purchased as souvenirs.

Colin Farrell (right) and Brendan Gleeson (left) star in the 2008 film 'In Bruges'

they are going, and find the place names completely unpronounceable. But miraculously, all are greeted by the Brugeans with a friendly smile and given well-considered information, even at the end of a busy summer season. If a conversation is struck up in a bar, it is quite usual for a tourist to be offered a drink – without one being expected in return.

Food & Drink in Bruges

Basically, there are three types of restaurant in Bruges: fast food outlets, tourist restaurants and luxury establishments. Only a few bars (or cafés as they are usually called) offer much in the way of food. Belgian cuisine, at its highest level, is basically French with a few local specialities incorporated. Some of the best food in the world is served in Belgian restaurants, and those who can afford their understandably high prices are recommended to have at least one 'gourmet' meal during their stay.

Whilst menus at the more expensive restaurants are usually written in French, astonishingly, many restaurants aimed primarily at tourists display menus outside their establishments in Dutch, a language that the vast majority of prospective customers do not understand. One can only presume that nationalism plays a part here as it certainly makes no commercial sense. Some may have noticed a similar attitude in Barcelona, where menus in the Catalan language are displayed to uncomprehending tourists. The only remedy seems to be to walk on, or demand to be shown a menu in English

or French.

Many will wish to take the opportunity of sampling Flemish specialities that are only available in Belgium. These are absolutely delicious, particularly the casseroles (*carbonades*) simmered in beer, but only generally available outside the summer months.

The great culinary feature of Bruges, also outside the summer months, is mussels – always, but always, served with a mountain of *frites* (chips). Whilst Belgians may eat mussels two or three times a year, it seems to be expected, at least in Markt, that tourists want to consume nothing else. Very few of the luscious molluscs will have ever been to the seaside, virtually all come from Holland where they are farmed in salt-water lakes, and can attain a huge size. Unfortunately, they do not seem to have quite the sweet, slightly fishy flavour of mussels from the open sea. No less than one kilogram weight per person is served.

Two Flemish favourites not to be missed are *Waterzooi*, a chicken or fish dish from Ghent prepared in a thick, rich white sauce. It is often served in two separate portions so that the dish remains hot. Equally delicious is wild rabbit simmered for around 90 minutes in white beer – *Konijn op grootmoeders wijze* (rabbit grandmother's style). Prunes or raisins are often cooked with the dish, but the only vegetables involved are onions; bread or even cake generously spread with mustard may be used to thicken the sauce. Do not allow chips to be served with this as they are a poor accompaniment; make it clear that boiled potatoes or bread are preferred. It is not usual to serve vegetables with this dish, but apple sauce is sometimes offered.

Carbonade a la Flamande is simply a casserole, usually of beef, to which beer is added. *Hutspot a la Flamande* involves vegetables and can be compared with a Lancashire hot-pot, although the meat is more likely to be beef than lamb. *Stamppot Ardennaise met Worst* is a thick stew served with spicy sausage – an Ardennes speciality that occasionally appears on Bruges menus. Although not a Flemish dish, *Blanquette de Veau* is extremely good in Belgium (for those who are not squeamish about eating veal). Cheese is rarely served in Bruges restaurants but, if the opportunity occurs, the brave should try *Herve*, a Belgian cheese that when ripe is one of the strongest in the world.

Desserts

For dessert, apple tart and chocolate mousse seem to be the most popular dishes or, of course, ice cream. Ice cream is very good in Bruges and, if bought in an ice cream shop, significantly cheaper than in the United Kingdom, or France for that matter. Also cheaper than elsewhere, although still expensive, are Belgian handmade chocolates, available in Bruges from many specialist shops. Try champagne truffles – the plain chocolate version is best.

Visitors who have enjoyed the seventeenth-century brown bars in

Amsterdam with their sanded floors, lofty ceilings and ancient barrels, will be disappointed to learn that the Bruges equivalents are far less venerable in appearance. Although the interiors of Bruges's better restaurants are exquisite, little attention is paid to decor in the bars. Perhaps beer drinking is considered too serious an exercise to bother with such frippery.

A list of recommended restaurants in various price categories is given in the FactFile.

Climate

The climate of Bruges is maritime, with no great extremes of temperature. It can rain at any time of the year, but winter rainfall tends to be low. Temperatures are generally slightly below those of southern England, as Flanders derives less benefit from the Gulf Stream.

1. Highlights of Bruges

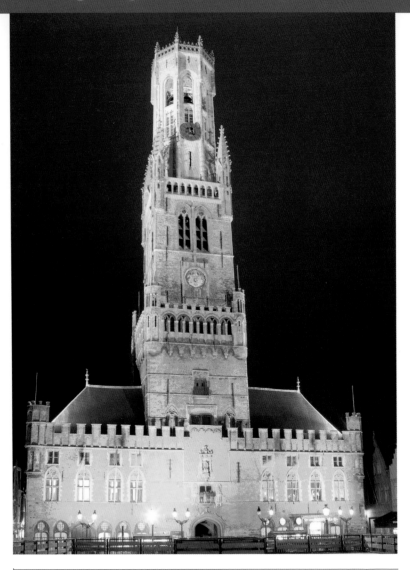

Route 1

Together with Paris and Amsterdam, Bruges has become one of the most popular 'City Break' short holiday destinations for British visitors. Most, therefore, have limited time available and, particularly if on a first visit, they may understandably wish to explore the city's highlights as soon as possible. Conveniently, many of these can be seen by following an almost straight line from the Markt/Burg axis southward towards the station, from where buses or taxis depart in the direction of most Bruges hotels.

The Belfry, Town Hall & Museums

Although the distance involved in following this route is little more than 2 km (1½ mile), there is so much to see that if some time is spent in all the museums and churches on route, it will be quite impossible to complete this 'itinerary' in one day. When the weather is fine and time permits, it might be a good idea to begin by exploring Markt and Burg thoroughly, as described, putting on one side the museums, including the famous Groeninge Museum, in case the weather deteriorates.

Four more important museums, plus the Church of Our Lady, cluster around the Groeninge, which will prove to be particularly advantageous on a rainy day. If at all possible, the Begijnhof and Minnewater, which follow, should be seen in fair weather.

Throughout the city will be seen the Gothic letter b, usually inscribed on stone plaques; this, of course, is the initial letter of Bruges, and many examples are extremely ancient.

Virtually all first-time visitors to Bruges make their way immediately to its largest square, Markt, in order to crane their necks at the belfry, rearing up from the south side. Actually, Markt (and similarly Burg) is angled north-west to south-east; this means that the belfry and the almost equally renowned town hall, only receive direct sunlight during the late afternoon, which is, therefore, the best time to photograph them.

Belfry history and exterior

Locals call the Belfry, Belfort or De Halletoren (The Hall Tower), but whatever it may be called, the 83m (272ft) high bell tower is hard to miss; thankfully, however, it is not quite so omnipresent as the postcards and picture books of Bruges might suggest.

At the foot of the belfry, the building known as Halle (Hall) originally served as a cloth hall; immediately below this ran a canal from which bales of cloth could be unloaded under cover. Modelled on Lakenhalle, a similar building at

Ypres, Halle was begun in the thirteenth century in early Gothic style, and from the outset incorporated a belfry. Initially, only the range of Halle facing Markt was built, its other three wings being added later.

The earliest belfry was probably made entirely of wood, but soon (circa 1240) a brick structure took its place. This, however, was struck by lightning in 1280, and the present belfry of stone was built between 1282 and 1296. It was bravely decided that the new, second stage should lean 1m (3ft) to the west, in order to counterbalance the lower level, which had already developed a similar lean to the east. The four corner turrets were added in 1395 as lookout points.

Designed in the late-Gothic style of Brabant, the octagonal lantern was added between 1482 and 1486, and surmounted by a decorative wooden spire. Destroyed by lightning in 1493, the spire was rebuilt in 1501 but burnt down again in 1741. This time, the lantern was left flat-topped – perhaps the insurance premiums demanded for yet another spire had become unacceptable! Eventually, in 1822, the present stone parapet was added.

There are four faces to the clock, the mechanism of which dates from 1680. Every quarter of an hour, tunes are played on the carillon, a comforting favourite for British tourists sometimes being *Land of Hope and Glory*. The belfry has long been, of course, the symbol of Bruges, its 'Eiffel Tower' so to speak, and most will have seen numerous photographs of it well before arriving. Not everyone has admired the belfry, however: G.K. Chesterton, for example, disparagingly compared

it with a giraffe's neck. Conversely, the American poet Longfellow praised the tower enthusiastically in a short poem dedicated to it. After a while in Bruges one gets used to the gawky structure peering unexpectedly through gaps in the roofline, rather like a spindly maiden aunt keeping a watchful but affectionate eye on her young nephews and nieces. This affection will soon be reciprocated.

The cobbled **Markt**, as its name suggests, was originally the most important market square in Bruges, and indeed it remained so from 985 until quite recently, when the Saturday market was transfered to 't Zand. Brugeans protested strongly, carrying black flags through the square on 27 August 1993, the day that the market finally closed. For a brief period this beautiful square became a municipal car park, but all vehicles were removed in 1996 and tranquillity has returned apart from Wednesday, when Markt accommodates, once more, a market (7am–1pm). It is in Markt that horse-drawn carriages may be hired from 10 am, except on Wednesdays, when they migrate to Burg.

The venerable Halle and its belfry occupy the entire south side of Markt, and virtually all the north side facing it similarly accommodates ancient buildings. Most of these were formerly the seventeenth-century guild houses of various trades.

They have been converted comparatively recently into tourist cafés and restaurants. **Le Panier d'Or** is surmounted by the basket emblem of the Tilers Guild. Further west, now **La Civière d'Or** restaurant, the castellated former house of the Fishmongers Guild is dated 1622: fish were sold outside the premises until 1745.

Many Brugeans stick their noses up at the Markt cafés, considering them far too tourist-orientated, both in price and quality, for them to patronize. Outside the summer months, it would appear that few patrons are expected to consume anything but mussels and chips. Many British are disconcerted by this combination which, incidentally, is also popular in Holland and France. If bread is preferred, it will of course be served, but the price quoted for mussels includes chips, and no reduction can be expected.

Brugean heros

Late nineteenth-century green **bronze statues** of two Brugean heroes, Jan Breydel, Dean of the Butchers Guild, and Pieter de Coninck, of the Weavers Guild (who led an amateur force in the uprising against the professional French army in 1302), stand in a small green towards the north end of the square. On the monument's pedestal, a frieze depicts the Bruges Matins of 18 May 1302, the Battle of the Golden Spurs 11 July 1302 and the Battle of the Pevelenberg, 1304. Corner sculptures represent the Belgian cities of Bruges, Ghent, Ypres and Kortrijk. Until demolished by anti-Christians during the French Revolution, the medieval church of St Christopher occupied an island site approximately where the monument now stands.

The east side of Markt is entirely pastiche Gothic, its three buildings being commissioned by the state. At the north end, built of grey sandstone (always referred to in Bruges as blue sandstone), the Burgundian Gothic style building, now the headquarters of the **Public Works Department**, only dates from the 1920s.

Much more impressive than the Public Works building is the gleaming white **Provincaal Hof**, the seat of the West Flanders Administration, designed in 1878 by Louis Delacenserie. He pinched several motifs from the Gruuthuse mansion, which he had restored, in particular its slender turrets, parapet and dormer windows. He seems also to have taken a liking to the Gothic finials of the Stadhuis, reproducing them almost exactly.

To the right of the Provincaal Hof in contrasting red brick, we have the main **post office** of Bruges. Before 1878 when it burnt down, a late-eighteenth-century, Louis XVI style range had occupied the site of these buildings. Prior to this, however, another cloth hall known as Waterhalle, stood here from 1294, so named because it had been built on a bridge over the Kraanrei Canal. The hall was demolished in 1787 and the arm of the canal filled: two of its columns survived and have been re-erected in Arentspark.

The west side of Markt is similarly dominated by Gothic Revival buildings. One, however, is genuine Gothic, although it looks even more modern than the others. This is **Huis Bouchoute** on the Sint Amandsstraat corner, a rectangular house built around 1480. Its façade, combining brick and grey paintwork, was restored in 1995, apparently with great fidelity, later roof top crenellations being removed. Still displayed is an octagonal compass; this was fitted to a weathervane on the

Route 1: Highlights of Bruges

| 0 | 50 | 100 | 150 | 200 | 250 metres |
| 0 | 50 | 100 | 150 | 200 | 250 yards |

Route 1

① Belfry
② Halle
③ Huis Bouchoute
④ Provincaal Hof
  (Provincial Government)
⑤ Post Office
⑥ Proostdij (Former Provost's House)
⑦ Tourist Information Centre
⑧ Provinciaal Museum
  het Brugse Vrije
⑨ Oude Griffie
  (Former Recorder's House)
⑩ Stadhuis (Town Hall)
⑪ Heilig Bloed Basiliek
  (Holy Blood Basilica)
⑫ Ter Steeghene (shopping mall)
⑬ Europacollege

⑭ Groeninge Museum
⑮ Arentshuismuseum/Lace Museum
⑯ Gruuthuse Museum
⑰ Arentspark
⑱ Onze-Lieve-Vrouwekerk or O-L-V
  (Church of our Lady)
⑲ Sint Janshospitaal
  (St John's Hospital) and
  Memling Museum
⑳ Godshuis Meulenaere and
  Godshuis Sint Jozef (almshouses)
㉑ Straffe Hendrik (brewery)
㉒ Godshuis De Vos (almshouses)
㉓ Begijnhof (almshouses)
㉔ Poertoren (Powder Tower)
㉕ Railway and Bus Stations
㉖ Diamant Museum

⬛ Walking route

Markt, the city's grandest square

roof in 1682 so that merchants would know the all-important wind direction prevailing.

Craenenburg

The Craenenburg café was built on part of the site of an eponymous medieval house which had a brief period of importance in Flemish history. Rioting citizens, furious at his tax impositions, placed Archduke Maximilian under house arrest within the building in February 1488. Allegedly, his captors commissioned the famous artist Gerard David to paint scenes on the shutters for Maximilian's pleasure, but there is no evidence for that. After twenty-two days, the Archduke was released on the promise of respecting the people's rights, but within a few weeks his father, Emperor Frederick III, marched into Flanders to exact revenge, moving the administrative centre from Bruges to Ghent and transferring much of the city's trade to Antwerp.

The café *(below)* boasts some attractive stained glass and brass chandeliers but, as is usual in the tourist sectors of Bruges, sitting (or standing) at the bar is not permitted.

An impressive façade distinguishes the adjoining **Huyze Die Maene** restaurant (*huyze* being the old Dutch spelling of *huis*, which means house). In spite of its venerable appearance, however, the building only dates from 1947.

Halle interior

Apart from the belfry and the courtyard of Halle, no interiors of the buildings in Markt are of exceptional interest. The ground floor rooms of Halle are frequently open to the public for art exhibitions, when entry to them is gained directly from Markt. Gothic vaulted ceilings survive within rooms, but there is little other detailing.

If the weather is clear, those who feel fit enough for a steep climb may now wish to ascend the belfry via the archway in the centre of Halle; from a balcony public announcements were made until 1769.

The Belfry Interior

Access to the Belfry is gained from the north gallery. There is no lift and the 366 steps, which spiral around the interior of the tower, must be climbed to reach the top – fortunately, there are resting stages. Those who have some misgivings about the safety of the structure on account of its double lean already referred to, will be relieved to know that columns were inserted in 1554 to give structural support, and no further movement has been observed.

Kept for centuries within a room called the *secreet comptoir* at the second stage of the belfry, now the museum, was a chest containing documents known as the Privileges of the City, in which the city magistrates spelled out the rights of the citizens of Bruges. So important were these privileges considered to be that the chest was protected by an ornate double grille, fitted with nine elaborate locks, the key to each being guarded by separate officials. It is known that the grille was made by a Brugean smith in 1292 specifically for the room, which had just been built.

Views of Bruges from the top of the belfry reveal the city in all its 'toy town' charm; they are usually at their clearest and most extensive in the late afternoon. On occasions it is possible to observe the Belgian coast to the west. Descend to the courtyard.

Halle courtyard

In the Middle Ages, Venetian merchants sold spices here. The side wings were added in 1365, but the south wing, which finally enclosed the trapezium-shaped courtyard, was not built until 1566, when the Renaissance style had taken over from the Gothic. This is why all galleries overlooking the courtyard are Renaissance work. In the south gallery, seats have been fitted so that the public may listen in comfort to the belfry's forty-seven-bell carillon concerts. It is considered that the bells are most clearly heard in Bruges from within this courtyard – no charge is made to attend.

The former cloth hall, on the first floor, is now used for private functions, and only rarely may the public gain admission. It was at one of these, the opening of the College of Europe's new term, 20 September 1988, that the guest speaker, Margaret Thatcher (then Prime Minister of the United Kingdom), spoke against European federalism, thus giving rise to the formation of the 'Bruges Group' of British Members of Parliament that shared her views.

Breidelstraat

A return through the arch from the courtyard into Markt followed by an immediate right turn leads to Breidelstraat, named, in spite of the updated spelling, to commemorate Jan Breydel, whose monument has just been seen in Markt. Between two shops at numbers 12 and 14 Breidelstraat, a quaint alleyway, leads to a small café, popular with tourists but of no particular interest apart from its sequestered location. At 24 Breidelstraat, **Breydel De Coninck**, is still regarded by many as the restaurant where the largest mussels in Bruges may be found.

On the north side (No 3 Burg), the former Proostdij van Sint Donaas (House of the Provost of Sint Donaas the first cathedral of Bruges), was constructed in the Flemish Baroque style in 1666. The building extends into the square known as Burg.

Burg

Pronounced Berha (roughly), Burg in Dutch means castle, and it was on part of the site of the present square that Boudewijn, the first Count of Flanders, constructed his fortress in 862. From its west end, by a bridge links Starhuis between street and with room over a narrow street with the Renaissance façade of the former Recorders House. Attached to the west side of the Stadhuis is the medieval Holy Blood Basilica; its fanciful entrance, together with the rest of the west range, is entirely pastiche Gothic.

Tours of Bruges by horse drawn carriages are begun nearby every Wednesday. Trees grow on the north side of Burg, but it was here that St Donaas Cathedral stood for centuries, until demolished by iconoclastic supporters of the French Revolution in 1792. The east side of the square is entirely occupied by a Classical complex of municipal buildings, eighteenth-century work but uninspired.

(Continued on p.28)

Stadhuis (Town Hall)

Proudly occupying most of the south side of Burg for almost 600 years is Stadhuis (Town Hall), the first municipal headquarters of its type, which was to influence the appearance of many similar structures in Belgium: those of Brussels, Ghent and Leuven being outstanding examples. Built between 1376 and 1420 of white sandstone, the façade is virtually an outdoor sculpture gallery, in which members of the nobility and biblical figures are depicted standing within niches beneath Gothic canopies.

It was the biblical figures in particular that infuriated the French revolutionaries, but just to be on the safe side, they smashed to pieces all the original forty. Originally, each example had been gilded and painted, the great Flemish artists living in Bruges at the time, including Van Eyck, probably contributing to their decoration. In the nineteenth century, replacements were made but the stone used proved too soft, and by 1960 most detail had 'melted' away. Its replacement were made in a vaguely Gothic style; canopies appear to be similar to the originals. The only nineteenth-century figure that was considered to be in good enough condition to keep stands on the far right of the façade. It will be noted that the present statues are undecorated, and the effect must be very different from the riot of colour that existed in medieval times. Stadhuis is entered primarily to admire its Gothic Hall, (see right) with the world-famous timber roof.

Large paintings of the rulers of Bruges and Flanders decorate the ground floor hall, from which a bluestone staircase leads to the Gotische Zaal (Gothic Hall) - see right.

Of the many important events in Flemish history that have taken place in this great room, the best known is the Assembly of the States General of the Netherlands, in 1464. Constructed in 1402, an unusual double vault has been employed in constructing the roof, both vaults being supported by stone corbels (also known as consoles or brackets). The vaults meet in the centre to form pendants, and thus provide a single span roof – quite an engineering feat.

Each of the sixteen corbels is carved to depict, respectively, the months of the year and the four elements; the bosses of the pendants illustrate Old Testament

scenes. It would appear that all the woodwork is original, but restoration of the gilding and paintwork has taken place periodically. Visitors will be given a leaflet that identifies the medieval events depicted in the hall's murals, which only date from around 1900.

In a side room are displayed ancient maps and topographical paintings of Bruges. Also on view are sections of the Stadhuis façade's original canopies, carved by Jean de Valenciennes, who is also believed to have been responsible for the decorative scheme of the Gothic Hall's roof.

Heilig Bloed Basiliek

(Holy Blood Basilica)

A left turn immediately after leaving the **Stadhuis** leads to the **Heilig Bloed Basiliek** (Holy Blood Basilica), the north wall of which adjoins Stadhuis. Originally, a narrow street separated the two buildings, but this disappeared when Stadhuis was extended across it in the fifteenth century.

Although short, the much-altered north wall of the basilica does much to illustrate the complex history of this relatively small church, the most ancient building in Bruges to survive. Since its construction in 1139, the basilica has always comprised two superimposed oratories. It is believed to have been founded as the chapel of the Counts of Flanders, whose residence stood nearby.

On completion, relics of St Basil, then kept in St Donaas church, were moved to it. They had been brought to Bruges from the Holy Land in 1100 by Count Robert II of Flanders who took part in the First Crusade. St Basil was venerated in the early Greek Church, and his relics (four vertebrae) were greatly valued. Their importance, however, was eclipsed in the following century by the arrival of an even more valued relic, a rock-crystal phial purported to contain blood washed from Christ's body at the Crucifixion by Joseph of Aramathea (the Holy Blood). It is now generally believed that this was despatched to Bruges circa 1204 by Boudewijn, Count of Flanders coming, who had been appointed Emperor of Constantinople that year.

Fronting Markt, the first section of the north wall of the basilica's lower oratory, now attached to Stadhuis, was formed in 1504 when a south chapel was added to the chancel for the exclusive use of lawyers. This is followed by a section of the original twelfth-century wall, with one Romanesque, round-headed window and part of another visible; a Lombard frieze has been entirely lost. The now blocked archway that opened out from the north aisle of the lower oratory into the square was created by iconoclasts during the French occupancy. At first floor level may be seen the Gothic windows of the upper oratory.

Originally, the entire church had been built in Romanesque style, but around 1480 it was decided to completely rebuild the upper oratory, the late-Gothic style being adopted for it. During the French Revolution period, the basilica was used for storage and became derelict; it is said that demolition was threatened but Napoleon intervened. By standing further back in the square, the unusual turrets of the basilica, which were built in the fifteenth century, come into view.

The large, arcaded porch was rebuilt in 1829, in picturesque neo-Gothic style. Entrance from here to the lower oratory is through the portal to the left, built in 1534.

Small windows and massive walls immediately announce that this is a Romanesque building. The nave is aisled but not the chancel, which is austerely provided with priest's seats (sedilia) fitted into blind arcades on both sides. The relics of St Basil, once displayed here, can no longer be seen they are now kept in the closed north chapel of the chancel built for the lawyers. In the south aisle of the nave, the Virgin and Child was carved in 1300.

A south chapel was added to the nave's south aisle in the thirteenth century and, surprisingly for the date, this was also built in a matching Romanesque style. Within is displayed a figure of the enthroned Christ, which is still carried in religious processions; it was made in the seventeenth century for Jeruzalemkerk.

An archway from the chapel to the south aisle is fitted with a Romanesque tympanum depicting a scene that probably illustrates the baptism of St Basil. This archway had been the priests' entrance to the church before its south chapel was added; their houses at the time abutted this side of the building.

The original public entrance to the basilica has also been relocated, as is indicated at the west end of the nave, where a blocked archway in the wall marks its original position. Access to this was from a street, which like that at the east end of the building, has since been built over.

Exit to Markt, turn immediately left and ascend the late-Gothic staircase, left, constructed in 1523, that leads to the upper oratory, where the crystal phial of holy blood is kept within a silver tabernacle presented by Albrecht and Isabella of Spain in 1611. On Fridays, the relic is moved to the south chapel where it may be venerated 8.30–11.45am and 3–4pm. The phial, within its gold reliquary, is paraded through the streets of Bruges on Ascension Day, a tradition confirmed by papal bull of Clement V in 1310. It is said that on the first Friday following the arrival of the relic in Bruges, the dried blood miraculously liquified; it continued to do so from time to time, always on a Friday, but the last recorded occasion was in 1325.

It may be noted that the three archways separating the south chapel from the nave are round-headed; they are genuine Romanesque work, all that remains of the original upper oratory. Little also remains of the Gothic reconstruction carried out in the late fifteenth century, due to damage caused during the French Revolution, which necessitated the rebuilding of the chancel in the late nineteenth century. Dating from this period are the heavy murals, but the pulpit, in the form of a globe, was carved from a single piece of oak in 1728.

Adjacent to the upper oratory is the Treasury, now a museum. Here is displayed the processional gold reliquary of the Holy Blood. It was made by Bruges goldsmith Jan Crabbe in 1617, and incorporates a diamond that is believed to have belonged to Mary Stuart of England, and the crown of Mary of Burgundy.

After descending to Burg, a left turn leads to **Mallebergplaats**, a small park created at the north end of the square. Trees and benches make this a pleasant spot in which to relax on a warm day. A bronze sculpture *The Lovers* is a reminder that civil weddings take place in Stadhuis, opposite.

The Lost Cathedral

Formerly, the park's area was occupied by part of the original cathedral of Bruges, dedicated to St Donaas. Rebuilt several times, the cathedral in its final form stretched eastward from the Provost's House to the north-east corner of Burg. It originated around 900 as a Carolingian church, which burnt down in 1184. A scale model in stone showing how it appeared, with its centrally placed, circular nave, has been erected in the park. An adjacent stone slab commemorates the alleged murder in its chancel of Count Charles the Good by a nephew of the cathedral's provost in 1127.

Part of the lower level of the church was excavated between 1931 and 1990, and incorporated within the basement of what is now the **Crowne Plaza Hotel**, overlooking the park. Visitors are welcome at any time to view the remains of the church, which are reached by descending the stairs to the left of the reception desk. It is helpful to examine the plan facing the bottom of

Late fifteenth century gothic detailing of the Basilica

the stairs before entering the excavated area. A painting of 1690 is displayed, depicting the large Gothic building that the small Romanesque church eventually became. In 1441, Jan van Eyck, the painter, was buried in Sint Donaas, which had not yet become a cathedral. During the period of the French Revolution, all churches were secularized but not necessarily destroyed if an alternative use for the building could be found. In this instance, the cathedral was sold as national property in 1792, but demolished 7 years later.

Municipal Offices

As already mentioned, the east side of Burg, comprising Municipal Offices, is not particularly distinguished, the sandstone building, commissioned by the Brugse Vrije, being the work, of an Amsterdam architect, Jan Verkruys, 1722–27. Brugse Vrije (Liberty of Bruges) was the administrative authority for the area of Flanders between the rivers Ijzer and Scheldt but excluding the city of Bruges itself. Old paintings depict a much more picturesque complex of buildings on the site, dating from the fifteenth century. Most were replaced by the eighteenth-century building. However, the rear façade, looking over the water, was spared and its Gothic gables are seen later. The French abolished the Brugse Vrije in 1795 but its buildings survived, becoming the Gerechsthof (Law Court) from the late eighteenth century until 1984, when it was relocated.

Oude Griffie

Linked to Stadhuis by the bridge-room over Blinde Ezelstraat, the façade

Tourist boats are only covered in wet weather

of Oude Griffie (former Recorder's House) is far more impressive, particularly after its colourful restoration in 2001. It was constructed by Jean Wallot (1535–37) to accommodate municipal records, and is an interesting architectural blend of Gothic and Renaissance. Medallions above the ground floor columns depict Flemish rulers, while at upper level, gilded statues of Justice flanked by Moses and Aaron are apparently accurate nineteenth-century

This corner of Burg houses, left to right: the Brugse Vrije, Oude Griffie and Stadhuis

reproductions of the originals, which were destroyed in 1792. Oude Griffie's rooms are not open to the public.

Provinciaal Museum Het Brugse Vrije

The doorway to the left of Oude Griffie leads to the **Provinciaal Museum Het Brugse Vrije**, accommodated within the court rooms, built 1520–25, that have survived from the Gothic complex. Major cases were tried in the Tribunal Room, now the hall, in which are displayed municipal items of historic value, but it is the Aldermen's Room, where minor cases were heard, that visitors come to see and for good reason, as it boasts one of the finest chimneypieces in the world.

Occupying more than a third of the wall space, this magnificent example of Flemish carving was worked on by various sculptors (1529–31) under the supervision of the Bruges artist Lancelot Blondeel. It was commissioned to celebrate the Treaty of Kamerrijk (1529), under which the vassal status of Flanders with the King of France was ended after 600 years. Charles V, Emperor of the Holy Roman Empire and Count of Flanders, had defeated François I at the Battle of Pavia in 1525, and an initial peace treaty was signed at Madrid the following year.

Although some Gothic elements can still be observed (in particular the coats of arms), the figures that dominate the piece are undoubtedly Renaissance in style, most of them being carved by Gugot de Beaugrant. Although oak is the prime material employed, black marble and alabaster can also be noted. As may be expected, the main figure is that of Charles V; he is flanked, to the right, by his maternal grandparents Ferdinand and Isabella of Spain and, to the left, by his paternal grandparents Maximilian of Austria (the archduke imprisoned in Craenenburg) and Mary of Burgundy. Behind Charles may just be seen portrait medallions of his parents, Philip the Fair and Joan the Mad (daughter of Ferdinand and Isabella). It would seem that the relegation of his parents to bust representation, together with their part concealment, indicates a wish on the part of Charles to hide them without completely disregarding their existence.

At upper level, even more difficult to identify, are portrait medallions of Charles de Launay, the general who led Charles V's army to victory at Pavia, and the Emperor's aunt, Margaret of Austria, by tradition a prime mover behind the scenes in negotiating the complicated Treaty of Kamerrijk.

Just to show that there were no hard feelings, a portrait medallion of the defeated King of France, François I, is carved to the left of Charles. To the right is a similar bust of the Emperor's sister, Eleanor of Austria, who married François as one of the conditions of the Treaty of Kamerrijk. By such manoeuvering, honour was maintained and loss of face minimised.

The Old Testament story of chaste Susanna is related in the alabaster frieze of the mantelpiece. In the first panel, while bathing naked, Susanna is surprised by two old men who intend to have their way with her, but she understandably refuses. Infuriated, the men bring charges of adultery against Susanna in court, the penalty for which is death. In the third panel, Daniel cross-examines the men; they are found to be lying, and Susanna is acquitted. In the last panel, the old men are stoned to death. Quite right too!

The linking Withdrawing Room, the former chapel, added in 1607, now the reading room of the City Archives, and the Orphans' Administration Office of 1666 are not open to the public but can often be glimpsed.

Ter Steeghene

Sensitively, the citizens of Bruges have disguised their modern shopping developments by planning them in the form of covered multi-storey malls set between parallel thoroughfares. Their entrances are kept narrow, thereby inflicting minimal visual disturbance on the ancient streets. One such development, Ter Steeghene (the alleyway), leads from the south-west corner of Burg (just right of the Holy Blood Basilica) to Wollestraat.

In general the shops in malls such as Ter Steeghene provide good quality merchandise, avoiding the tattiness found in so many developments of this type in other countries.

Wollestraat

At Wollestraat (Wool Street), a left turn leads southward in the direction of the city's most important museums.

Located on the main tourist beat, most of Wollestraat's establishments understandably cater for their needs with lace, souvenirs, chocolates, ice creams and fast food restaurants predominating.

Numbering on the east side begins at Markt (odd numbers), but even

numbers, on the west side, do not commence until the street called Oude Burg has been passed. This is because the **east façade of Halle** occupies the entire block. Constructed in 1365, it may be observed that the upper courses of bricks have been completely renewed, eliminating the picturesque battlements, which originally matched those of the existing Markt façade.

A lace shop at **number 9** has been designed in Gothic Revival style; protruding from its façade is an oriel window behind which a mechanical model of a bonneted lacemaker 'works'. In Bruges until a few years ago many bonneted elderly ladies could be observed sitting outside their doorways making lace in fine weather, but they are now a rare sight. This was not done primarily for the benefit of tourists, but to gain as much natural light as possible so that eye strain would be kept to a minimum.

A short alleyway leads eastward from number 35 Wollestraat, opening up to form a small unnamed square overlooking the canal. Several restaurants take advantage of the idyllic views: 't **Traptje** is recommended for its hearty Flemish casseroles.

From 1578 to 1584, the large Gothic house at **number 53** Wollestraat accommodated the relic of the Holy Blood. Steps beside the house lead down to one of the many canal boat boarding stages.

On the opposite side of the road, lunettes on the ground floor of 28, a house built in 1634, are decorated with now rather faded polychrome bas-reliefs illustrating the siege of Bruges by Prince Frederik of Nassau's Protestant army in 1613.

Nepomucenusbrug with its monument to the eponymous Czech Saint

De Steen (The Stone), a high, circular tower, was built at the south end of Wollestraat, on the bridge corner, in the eleventh century. This is believed to have served as a residence of the counts of Flanders until Bruges ceased to be their base around 1400. The tower then became a prison until fire destroyed most of it in 1689. Only partly restored, all traces of the building were removed in 1785.

Nepomucenusbrug

Ending Wollestraat is the brick-built bridge Nepomucenusbrug; its name commemorates the Czech St John of Nepomucen, a fourteenth-century Canon of Prague and court chaplain. By tradition, he refused to reveal the confessions of Queen Sophie to her husband, King Wenceslas IV, and was martyred by being thrown from a bridge into the River Moldau. To commemorate his drowning the saint was frequently depicted on European bridges in the Middle Ages.

If the sun is shining, keen photographers may now, rather than later, wish to turn immediately left along **Rozenhoedkaai**, from where the world-famous view of the belfry is obtained (see page 64).

In order to reach the museum area, however, it is necessary to follow the canal in the opposite direction, along **Dijver**, a not particularly interesting street of patricians classical houses. Amongst the trees on the canal side there is a flea market Saturdays and Sundays, from 10am–6pm, March to November, when the sedate thoroughfare livens up. **Den Dijver Café**, at number 5, boasts a terrace where, in summer, snacks and beverages are served: ice creams and pancakes are deservedly popular. Internally, the restaurant is quite delightful; Flemish specialities are given inventive touches.

Europacollege

Europacollege (College of Europe) at number 9/11 Dijver has been located in Bruges since 1949. In spite of the name, its students come from many countries, their arrival adding a more cosmopolitan and youthful element to the city, which had been greatly needed since the demise of Bruges in the fifteenth century. The college specializes in postgraduate courses, being particularly strong in European-orientated law and economics.

Groeninge Museum

Many will find the **Groeninge Museum**, with its world-famous collection of Flemish Primitive paintings just about perfect in size and presentation – for once, the visitor leaves a great museum without feeling satiated. This is the only museum of importance in Bruges not to be located in an ancient building; an advantage of this is that the structure was designed specifically for the collection, which it has housed since 1930. It occupies the site of Eekhout Abbey, which was suppressed during the French Revolution and demolished in 1796. The name Groeninge commemorates the plain outside Kortrijk where the Flemish army defeated the French at the battle of the Golden Spurs in 1302.

All exhibits are captioned in four languages and sympathetically illuminated. Donations and acquisitions have meant that the Groeninge now possesses far more paintings than it has space to exhibit; works, therefore, are periodically rotated so that all are displayed at some time. Masterly detail and serene expressions vie with macabre scenes of horror that make the nastiest 'video nasty' seem like *Mary Poppins* in comparison. Glowing colours, with no sign of cracks, emphasise that the techniques of the Flemish Primitives were in no way primitive. It is hard to believe that most paintings on display are more than 500 years old.

On occasions, the permanent collection is replaced by special exhibitions.

Always exhibited (apart from special exhibitions) are two paintings by Van Eyck: *Portrait of the painter's wife, Margareta*, and *The Madonna with Canon van der Paele* altarpiece (illustrated on p. 38). Margareta was 33 years old when painted by her husband; such portraits were rare at the time, when almost all paintings had religious themes. By the

look of the sitter, however, it would have been a brave man who refused to paint her if she so commanded. The Van de Paele altarpiece was commissioned for the donor's private chapel in Sint Donaas Cathedral. St George and St Donaas are depicted on the right.

Not to be missed is the anonymous *Portrait of Lodewijk van Gruuthuse*, whose mansion now forms the Gruuthuse Museum. On his chain he wears the emblem of the Order of the Golden Fleece.

The Martyrdom of St Hippolytus is an important triptych by Dirk Bouts and Hugo Van der Goes, whilst *Death of the Virgin* is entirely the work of Van der Goes.

Memling's *Moreel triptych* is this artist's most important work at the Groeninge; six additional masterpieces by this painter are displayed in the Memling Museum (See page 48-50).

Those of a nervous disposition should visit room 6 with some trepidation, particularly on approaching the double-panelled *Judgement of Cambyses* by Gerard David, commissioned for the Aldermens' Room at Stadhuis in 1498. Cambyses, a Persian king, orders the arrest of a judge accused of corruption who is found guilty in the first panel. In the second, the King's sentence is carried out – flaying alive. Stretched out on a table while his body is expertly skinned, the face of the guilty judge is supposed to be modelled on that of Pieter Lanchals, executed in Bruges 10 years earlier. A rather more serene work by the same painter, *Baptism of Christ*, hangs in the gallery.

Perhaps most gruesome of all is the *Last Judgement* by Hieronymus Bosch,

Lace

It will be impossible to miss the lace shops in Bruges, and many will also wish to visit the Lace Museum and the Lace Centre, where the skilful lace makers can be observed at work. Although a primitive type of lace has been found in Ancient Egyptian tomb chambers, lace in its modern form was a European invention. The chief difference between lace and embroidery, which it resembles, is that lace is an ornamental fabric in itself, not an addition to one that already exists. There are two basic techniques – needlepoint, which is extremely difficult and was probably invented in Italy in the fifteenth century, and bobbin lace which also involves great skill in its more elaborate forms. On occasion, needlepoint and bobbin methods are combined.

Until 1800, the thread used in lace making was almost always flax (linen), although silk, metal and even fine wool were occasionally employed. After 1800, however, cotton thread began to be used more extensively than linen due to its lower cost – but the results were never quite as spectacular.

Bobbin lace probably evolved in Flanders in the early sixteenth century, to cope with the demand for lace trim to both men's and women's clothing. Late fifteenth-century Italian and Flemish portraits show hems and seams trimmed with lace, and by 1600 the lace industry was of great importance in western Europe. France, particularly north-west France, in addition to Flanders and Italy, was a large producer, and lace was also made commercially in Spain, Germany and England where Nottingham lace, in particular, gained an enviable reputation.

By the nineteenth century, lace had fallen completely out of fashion with men, and even women were wearing little of it. All was to change around 1840, however, when fashion did a complete turnabout and lace was once again in vogue – but for women only. Mechanical methods were introduced, cotton completely replaced flax thread, and the design standards fell. It was not until 1920 that lace would completely disappear from the fashion scene, but this time its demise in this market would appear to be final, with the exception of trim for ladies underwear. Lace is still made in Europe, particularly Bruges and Burano, Italy, now primarily for souvenirs such as doylies, and trim for linen articles. China, Taiwan and South-East Asia are also producers.

The first lace-making school in Bruges was founded by three nuns from Antwerp, in the early years of the eighteenth century. There was so little employment in Bruges at the time that lace-making soon became a popular means by which poor women could earn a living. Prices paid by the merchants were not high however fine the work, and many toiled for too many hours in order to make a living. In consequence their eyesight suffered, and many an elderly lacemaker became partially or even completely blind. It was not long before the inventions of the Industrial Revolution were to be applied to lace-making, and handmade bobbin lace then became no more than a part-time activity.

Only tourist demand has preserved the lace industry in Bruges; the skills of the ladies who make it are demonstrated at the Lace Centre in Peperstraat where items are for sale. Elsewhere, purchasers of lace in Bruges must beware factory-made imports from South-East Asia. Typical Bruges 'Duchesse' lace, produced from either thin or thick thread, is designed in delicate floral patterns. Up to 200 bobbins are employed in Point de Fee, the most exquisite of all Bruges lace. Genuine Bruges lace must display a Quality Control label: the Tourist Office will provide a list of outlets where it is guaranteed to be genuine.

a surrealist nightmare of demons and goblins designed to impress that hell was not the best of places in which to spend eternity.

Arentshuismuseum

The **Arentshuismuseum** occupies an eighteenth century mansion that straddles the canal. The price of admission covers the displays of lace, and paintings by Frank Brangwyn.

Lace display

Located on the ground floor, the lace display is based on the collection donated by Baroness Liedts. The evolution of 'Van Dijck' bobbin lace from the seventeenth century is demonstrated. Exhibits include needlepoint work from France and Italy in addition to Flanders. It will be noted that, with age, lace gradually becomes cream in colour, a helpful but not necessarily infallible sign of authenticity. Most will be impressed by the copy of a full-length painting of Empress Maria Theresa dressed in Brussels lace, the work of the Bruges artist Matthias de Visch dating from around 1750.

Brangwyn Collection

A staircase gives access from the hall to the **Frank Brangwyn Collection**. The artist was born at Bruges in 1867, but his Welsh father, William Brangwyn, took the family to England when the boy was only ten years old. Nevertheless, Frank Brangwyn obviously retained a great affection for the city of his birth, and presented this collection of his work to Bruges in 1936 *"as a memorial of my love for your great city"*.

Brangwyn is best known for his romantic oil paintings which at their best, can be reminiscent of Delacroix, with their brilliant colours and sinuous forms. At Bruges, however, most of the work displayed is graphic; etchings of the Begijnhof and Jan Van Eyckplein bearing witness to Brangwyn's return visits to Bruges.

The artist was certainly influenced by contemporary trends, noteworthy being the Art Nouveau character of some of his ex libris designs and the carpet, *De Wingerd* (Vineyard), of 1897. Examples of wooden furniture designed by Brangwyn are displayed throughout the galleries, most of them being Art Deco in style.

Two large oil paintings, *Slave Market* and an allegorical *British Empire* are perhaps the most important works on display. The latter was one of a set commissioned for the Royal Gallery of the House of Lords, Westminster, by Lord Iveagh, and painted between 1925 and 1930. Hung experimentally in the House of Lords for a short time, the works were eventually rejected as being 'too modern' for the building. Late nineteenth-century watercolours of Tangier and Egypt are valuable topographical records in addition to being examples of Brangwyn's skill in that medium. Frank Brangwyn died at Ditchling, Sussex, in 1956.

Opposite the entrance to the museums, and visible through large windows, is a collection of ancient coaches and sledges.

Arentspark

A pathway leads southward from the museum to Arentspark, formerly the

(Continued on p.40)

Flemish Primitives

The Flemish Primitives are definitely not a semi-naked tribe inhabiting a steamy Belgian jungle, but the name coined in the nineteenth century to define the earliest paintings of the Flemish School. No one is quite certain precisely what 'primitive' referred to; it may have meant 'the first', or it could have been an allusion to the artists' ignorance of the use of perspective and accurate proportions. Both the Groeninge and the Memling museums in Bruges are internationally renowned for their collections of these great works.

All Flemish Primitive masters are famed for their brilliant colours, meticulous, almost pedantic attention to detail, and the adoption of landscape backgrounds that give the illusion of depth. It was Philip the Good, Duke of Burgundy (1419-67), who, on transferring his court from Dijon to Bruges, brought with him the finest painters in his dukedom. Pre-eminent was **Jan Van Eyck**, (locally pronounced Yan Fan Ache) whom he employed in 1425 as peintre at valet de chambre. Some believe that Van Eyck invented oil painting, but this now seems unlikely. However, no other painter of any period has been able to match Van Eyck's technique; his colours remain as fresh and brilliant as the day they were first applied. Van Eyck's Virgin with Canon van der Paele can be seen in the Groeninge Museum, and not far from Bruges, in Ghent's Sint Baafskathedraal, is Van Eyck's masterpiece, the triptych known as The Adoration of the Mystic Lamb. The painter was born at Maaseik around 1395 and died at Bruges in 1441, having lived for many years in his house near Sint Gilliskerk. He was buried in Sint Donaas Cathedral.

Undoubtedly the greatest painting in Bruges is the Van Eyck altarpiece of The Madonna with Canon van der Paele. Its colours are as fresh as when they were painted almost 500 years ago

Because of the Memling Museum, most visitors to Bruges associate **Hans Memling** more closely than any other artist with the city, and he did spend much of his life here, dying at Bruges in 1494. Memling painted primarily religious subjects, but also portraits, being particularly fond of diptychs, in which one panel featured a Madonna and Child and the other the patron, often accompanied by his or her patron saint. The panels could be folded and were therefore easy to transport; few now remain in their double-panel state. Memling was the most prolific of all the Flemish Primitives, but some have noted a bland quality in his paintings, in spite of their technical brilliance. The painter's most famous work, the Shrine of St Ursula, is displayed in the Memling Museum.

Hugo van der Goes (c1440-1482) may have been born in Bruges but this is uncertain. At the age of 27 he was accepted as a master in the Painter's Guild of Ghent, where he gained many commissions. Charles the Bold certainly held Van der Goes in high esteem, as he placed him in charge of the decoration of Bruges to celebrate his marriage. In 1475, Van der Goes entered a convent near Brussels, where he is believed to have become mentally unstable, even, so it is said, attempting suicide. His work was certainly disturbing, as will be noted in the Groeninge Museum's Death of the Virgin, completed shortly before his own demise. The bright colours are unreal and, combined with the grieving expressions of the Disciples, create a sense of unease. It is considered that the masterpiece of Van der Goes is his Portinari triptych, commissioned by the Medici representative in Bruges. It is, in fact, the only fully documented work by the artist, and can be seen in the Uffizi, Florence.

Petrus Christus (1415-1472), who was working in Bruges three years after the death of Van Eyck, painted in a similar style to the master. One panel of a triptych, Isabella of Portugal (possibly) with Saint Elizabeth, is in the Groeninge collection.

Gerard David (c1460-1523), came to Bruges from what is now Holland, and lived many years in the city. His gruesome diptych, The Judgement of Cambyses, commissioned in 1498 for the Stadhuis in Burg, is a major attraction at the Groeninge Museum, although his Baptism of Christ triptych, usually in the same gallery, is considered by many to be a finer work.

Dirk Bouts (1415-75) was the first Flemish painter to adopt Renaissance techniques for creating an illusion of depth through single point perspective and the accurate proportioning of figures to other objects. Perhaps he should not really be defined as a Primitive.

The end of the Burgundian dukedom coincided with the decline of Bruges, and the two events heralded a fall in the quality of Flemish painting. In the sixteenth century, only **Hieronymus Bosch** (1450-1516) and **Pieter Breughel** (1529-69), both, in effect, early Surrealists, can be regarded as Flemish masters of great importance. More than a century was to pass before the Baroque works of the Antwerp School, led by **Rubens** and **Van Dyck**, would restore greatness to Flemish painting.

grounds of the Gruuthuse mansion, which is located on the opposite side of the canal. In the park have been erected two stone columns from the thirteenth-century Waterhalle which stood on the east side of Markt until demolished in 1787. Facing them are bronze equestrian figures representing the Knights of the Apocalypse: death, war, famine and revolution, the work of sculptor Rik Poot, 1987. From the west bank of the park there is an attractive view over the canal to the Gruuthuse courtyard.

The romantic Bonifacius bridge

Crossing the waterway to Gruuthuse and Onze-Lieve-Vrouwekerk is **Bonifacius brug**, the most picturesque bridge in Bruges, although the present hump-backed structure only dates from 1910. Seen from the bridge, looking back to the small building attached to it, is a venerable waterside inn sign of stone carved with a boat; it was brought here from Nieuwpoort. Outstanding external views of the chancel of Onze-Lieve-Vrouwekerk are gained from here.

Immediately left of Bonifacius Bridge, on the opposite bank of the canal, is a **bust of Joan Luis Vives** (1492–1540), a Catalan from Valencia who lived many years in Bruges where he met fellow humanists Erasmus and Sir Thomas More. Vives worked strenuously to relieve the condition of the poor in Flanders.

Immediately right, after the bridge has been crossed, rises the bare brick rear wall of the Gruuthuse mansion, bare that is apart from an exquisite little Gothic double window dating from

around 1470. The street leading to the mansion, Onze-Lieve-Vrouwe-Kerkhof Noord, branches right, whereas that branching left, Onze-Lieve-Vrouwe-Kerkhof Zuid, is more convenient for tentering Michelangelo's *Virgin and Child* sculpture may be seen. It should be borne in mind that its chancel is closed between 11.30am and 2.30pm.

On route to the church, two houses at **numbers 6 and 8**, built around 1904, are splendid examples of Art Nouveau work. Although Europe's finest architectural examples of this style, which is also known as Jugendstil (German), are to be found in Brussels, little was built in Bruges.

Onze-Lieve-Vrouwekerk

For many, **Onze-Lieve-Vrouwekerk** (Church of Our Lady), often understandably abbreviated to O-L-V, will be the first church visited in Bruges. Due to the absence of stone quarries in the vicinity, all were built of brick, which in fact, weathers better than stone. It does, of course, preclude carving, and external decoration is usually restricted to ribs of brick curved to form Gothic tracery, or in strips, to add delicacy and apparent height to structures. The present church was begun in the thirteenth century and completed in the fifteenth century. Much of its design, particularly that of the chancel and west towers, is reminiscent of Tournai Cathedral, the early-Gothic style of which was itself influenced by the great structures of northern France. Two earlier churches, both Romanesque, had previously occupied the site, the first of which is believed to have dated from the ninth century.

The great spire of the church is 122m (400ft) high and would still be the world's highest structure of brick masonry if Antwerp Cathedral's spire had not eclipsed it by just 1m (3ft) in 1518 – perhaps someone at Antwerp had a divine revelation that the *Guinness Book of Records* would eventually make an appearance! Work began on the spire in the thirteenth century and was completed by 1350; the present top section, however, is a fifteenth-century addition. In 1465, a late-Gothic portal of white stone was added to the north side of the tower. Known as Paradijsportaal (Gateway to Paradise), it is no longer an entrance, but has been fitted to serve as an oratory chapel which has served as a baptistery.

Onze-Lieve-Vrouwekerk is usually entered from the south portal. It is interesting to note that the triforium arcade of the nave is round-arched in Romanesque style while above this, the slightly larger clerestory windows are pointed in the Gothic manner, possibly a measure of the construction progress as taste changed. The nave's most notable furnishing is its Baroque eighteenth-century pulpit.

Most will now make for the south aisle, at the east end of which, set within a niche of black marble, is the *Virgin and Child* by Michelangelo (1475–1564), (See box on p. 42) sculpted in contrasting white marble. For reasons of security, it is not permitted to approach the masterpiece too closely, and only those with binoculars will be able to fully appreciate the serenity of the Virgin's expression. A balustrade is conveniently

placed on which cameras may be rested, thus avoiding the necessity for fast film, flash or a tripod in order to take successful photographs of the work when the light is reasonable.

The Chancel
(Chapel of Charles & Mary)

A charge is made for entering the chancel and its ambulatory (from the south side).

In 1468, the eleventh Chapter of the Order of the Golden Fleece was convened in the chancel to celebrate the third marriage of Charles the Bold, Duke of Burgundy, this time with Margaret of York, sister of England's King Edward IV who had become a close and grateful friend. The fifteenth-century coats of arms of the knights attending the ceremony have survived, that of Edward IV being above the front stall on the north side; the stalls themselves date from the eighteenth century.

In front of the high altar is a triptych *Passion*, most of it painted between 1534 and 1561 by Bernard van Orley of Brussels, although completed by Marcus Gerards.

Royal tombchests

Behind the altar are the gilded tombchests of Charles the Bold and his daughter, Mary of Burgundy. Although Mary died in 1482, five years after her father, her tomb was made earlier. She met her death, aged 24, falling from a horse whilst hunting with falcons. Archduke Maximilian of Austria, her husband, grieved *"Never, as long as I live, will I forget this faithful woman"*. The recumbent tomb figure of Margaret of

Bonifacius Bridge, the most picturesque in Bruges

years later, Charles V ordered that his great-grandfather's remains should be transferred to Bruges, but by the time they arrived — after a mysterious three-year sojourn in Luxembourg — Charles V had abdicated. It was left to his son and successor, Philip II, to commission a suitable tomb, which was designed by Jacob Jonghelinck of Antwerp. Charles the Bold's slogan, which may be translated as *"I have made the venture, may it prosper"*, is inscribed on the tomb. His recumbent figure is similar in style to that of Mary.

York was cast by Renier van Thienen and gilded by a Bruges goldsmith.

The tombchest of Charles the Bold lies beside that of his daughter, on which its design is modelled. Charles was killed during the siege of Nancy in 1477, but it was several days before what was believed to be his mutilated body was discovered in a frozen pond and interred at Nancy. Eighty-three

Between the tombchests and the altar, visible below ground level through glass, are examples of thirteenth- and four-teenth-century open tombs, their inner sides painted with religious themes in a manner that calls to mind the religious beliefs of the Ancient Egyptians. All were discovered in 1979.

Michelangelo's Virgin and Child

The sculpture was commissioned by Sienna Cathedral in Tuscany, but funds had run out by the time the work was finished in 1505, and a Brugean merchant of Italian descent, Jan Moscroen, was able to purchase it the following year. In 1514, the city treasurer of Bruges presented the piece to the church, where it has remained ever since. Apart from an expedition to Paris during the French Revolution and another to Germany in World War II, said to be the only piece of work by Michelangelo to leave Italy during his lifetime.

Michelangelo's Virgin and Child

Gruuthusestraat

The Lanchals chapel

Against the wall of the ambulatory's Lanchals chapel stands the black tombchest of Pieter Lanchals, decorated on its face with his swan emblem; *lanchals* in Dutch means long-neck, and the emblem was therefore a pun – a common practice at the time. Lanchals was executed at Markt in 1488 for 'treacherously' supporting Maximilian of Austria's tax increases on the Bruges citizens. By tradition, the introduction of swans to the city's canals was ordered so that Brugeans would be constantly reminded of their mistreatment of Lanchals. A municipal official in addition to being an adviser of Maximilian, Lanchals resided in a large house in Oude Burg, part of which still exists.

Gruuthuse chapel

In 1472, Lodewijk van Gruuthuse built a lower and an upper chapel for the exclusive use of his family. The lower chapel, now closed, provided direct entrance to the north ambulatory, while even greater privacy could be obtained from the oratory above as it was linked via a bridge over O.L.V. Kerkhof Noord with his mansion. Inscribed on the structure, *Plus est en vous* (More is in you) was the motto of Lodewijk, apparently a reference to the exhortation that he gave his troops in battle. Although only the oriel window of the chapel may be glimpsed from the north ambulatory of the church, visitors to the **Gruuthuse Museum** may enter it.

Gruuthuse Museum

After leaving the church, turn right into Gruuthusestraat which fronts the museum. Before entering the courtyard, which is free of charge, it is as well to admire the stone frieze depicting battle scenes, which decorates the external wall of the outhouse. This is genuine fifteenth-century carving, unlike most of the other architectural features of Gruuthuse which are nineteenth-century pastiche Gothic, the over-enthusiastic work of restorer

Onze-Lieve-Vrouwekerk's tower is the world's second highest brick structure

Louis Delacenserie. Right of the court-yard's entrance is the former stable block, now a tearoom.

Eventually, Gruuthuse became the L-shaped mansion which is now seen, but it evolved from the two-storey step-gabled house on the right. This was built in 1425 by Jan van Gruuthuse, who fixed the coat of arms of himself and his wife to the gable. The two identical Gothic balustrades of stone above the first floor windows are original.

Jan's son Lodewijk added the bridging oratory chapel to his father's house in 1472, but prior to this (1465–70) he had greatly extended the original building by the addition of two further ranges, forming the present L shape.

By the sixteenth century, Bruges had become an unfashionable address, well into its 'Rip Van Winkel' period, and Gruuthuse remained empty until 1628, when a charitable lending bank, Mons Pietas, took over the premises. Banks charging low interest rates, sometimes none at all, had been founded in Italy to break the monopoly of the Lombards' whose rates were extortionate, and similar establishments were set up in Flanders by Archduchess Isabella. The Dutch word *Mons* (Mountain) was a mistranslation of the Italian *Monte* (Money).

Dilapidation and restoration

By the nineteenth century, the Gruuthuse mansion had become a dilapidated pawnbroker's store; it was rescued by being chosen as the venue for the collection of Flemish antiques put together by local enthusiasts, which included British exiles William Brangwyn and John Steinmetz. Louis Delacensier was given the task of converting the house to a museum, which he began in 1892. It seems that apart from the kitchen and the oratory chapel, most original Gothic features had already been lost, and the architect added his own Gothic Revival work, a common late nineteenth-century solution throughout northern Europe. Apart from the two rooms mentioned, therefore, the picturesque fireplaces, balustrades and carvings throughout are relatively modern work.

The varied collection of antiques displayed throughout Gruuthuse includes tapestries, musical instruments, furniture, altarpieces, ceramics and coins. Look out for the famous painted bust of Charles V, attributed to Konrad Meit. It was made of terracotta in 1520 but decorated later.

An amusing painting of a baby being washed demonstrates that the procedure included giving the poor infant an enema.

Most impressive is the great kitchen and, on the upper floor, the oratory, added by Lodewijk van Gruuthuse to his father's house. From its window can be seen the sanctuary of Onze-Lieve Vrouwekerk. An enchanting view of Bonifacius Bridge is gained from the loggia.

Guido Gezelleplein

Facing the entrance to the Gruuthuse Museum is Guido Gezelleplein, named to commemorate the most famous Flemish poet, a priest, who lived from 1830 to 1899. Gezelle's statue, erected in 1930 to commemorate the centenary of his birth, is the work of Jules Lagre. The poet's birthplace, now a museum, may be visited in north Bruges.

The Gruuthuse family

The Gruuthuse family's name, in addition to its wealth, came from gruut, the Dutch word for grout, a secret combination of dried plants that was used by brewers to flavour beer before the introduction of hops. In the thirteenth century, the family was granted the right to levy a duty on all grout used by the brewers of Bruges, and they changed their name from Van Brugghe-van der Aa to Gruuthuse.

Lodewijk van Gruuthuse became one of the wealthiest and most important men in the Netherlands; his inumerable titles, awarded by Charles the Bold, whose marriage with Mary of Burgundy he had helped arrange, included: Knight of the Order of the Golden Fleece, Governor of Holland, Zeeland and West Friesland, and Commander of the Burgundian military forces. Lodewijk developed a close relationship with King Edward IV, supporting him financially in his successful efforts to regain the throne of England in the final stage of the Wars of the Roses. During his brief exile from England, Edward stayed at Gruuthuse from October 1470 to April 1471, accompanied by his apparently faithful brother Richard. This was the man who would later be crowned King Richard III, and later still be branded by William Shakespeare and the majority of historians as the monster who murdered his brother Edward's two young sons in the Tower of London.

As a reward for Lodewijk's assistance, Edward appointed him Earl of Winchester on regaining his throne. When Lodewijk, a patron of the arts, died in 1492, he had amassed an exceptional collection of illustrated manuscripts, but his son, who allied himself with France, left Bruges for Abbeville and sold the collection, which now forms part of the archives of the Bibliothèque Nationale in Paris.

Gruuthusestraat continues westward joining Mariastraat to the left, where, on the west side, a range of ancient buildings form Sint Janshospitaal, within which the Memling Museum and Bruges Tourist Office are located.

Sint Janshospitaal

Sint Janshospitaal (St John's Hospital) was founded around 1150 on the west bank of the river, which then marked the eastern boundary of Bruges. It is one of Europe's most ancient hospices, and was still serving as an infirmary in the nineteenth century. Only fragments of the twelfth-century structure have survived.

Five linked but distinct buildings form the Mariastraat façade. From right to left these are: **the cloister,** circa 1300, with an entrance archway; an early thirteenth-century **tower** with Romanesque windows; the **hospital's chapel,** built in Gothic style in the early thirteenth century; a **Romanesque ward,** early thirteenth century but with a porch added in 1900; its portal's thirteenth-century tympanum, depicting the *Death and the Coronation of the Virgin,* was augmented by the large roundel, made in 1900; finally, the **Gothic ward** was built in 1315.

The complex is entered through the porch and the visitor is immediately impressed by the hospital's great open spaces and soaring arches. Restoration of some of the wards to their appearance when in use was considered but rejected as being too kitsch – perhaps the administrators had been appalled by the Disney-like appearance of the recently restored rooms in the Tower of London! An eighteenth-century painting of the hospital's interior is seen later.

Excavation has revealed the foundations of the hospital's first, twelfth-century, chapel that has been preserved *in situ.*

In deference to the patients that died in the wards, many of whom were interred beneath their floors, the area will not be used for temporary exhibitions or functions as had been initially proposed. However, a large area at upper level will provide facilities for these. Against the end wall is displayed a copy of the façade's tympanum. Note the splendid thirteenth-century truss roof.

On entering the former **chapel** note that the blocked archways of the south wall were originally open to the adjoining ward; dying and very sick patients could therefore celebrate Mass without leaving their beds.

Memling Museum

The museum is housed in the former chapel, and comprises six works by Hans Memling, who was born between 1435 and 1440 at Seligenstadt, a pros-

Gruuthusemuseum - former palace of the Lords of Gruuthuse (15th century)

perous German town near Frankfurt. He is known to have been in residence at Bruges by 1465. Bruges was then at the height of its importance, and the young painter received many commissions from wealthy merchants and diplomats visiting the city; for this reason, his works are distributed widely amongst European collections. Eventually, Memling must have amassed quite a fortune for the time, as he is known to have owned three houses in the city. He died at Bruges in 1494.

Shrine of St Ursula

Displayed first is the world-famous *Shrine of St Ursula.* This was made to

Memling, a hospital patient?

There is an unlikely tradition that Memling had been wounded at the Battle of Nancy in 1477, fighting for Charles the Bold, whom he certainly knew, and that he was cared for at Sint Janshospitaal. If true, it would explain how the brothers and sisters had been able to afford to commission four works from such a famous and presumably expensive painter. All were completed within the three years that followed the Battle of Nancy, and, as has been said, Memling depicted a patient of the hospital, possibly himself, in the Adoration of the Magi triptych.

contain relics of the Saint in the possession of the hospital, and commissioned by two of its sisters around 1480. Made of gilded wood, the reliquary is entirely Gothic in style. One of the painted panels depicts the two sisters who commissioned the work kneeling before the Virgin Mary.

Like so many Christian legends, that of St Ursula dates from the thirteenth century. Believed to be a princess from Brittany, Ursula consented to marry a pagan king if he converted to Christianity and sent her, accompanied by other virgins, on a pilgrimage to Rome to receive the Pope's blessing. On their return journey the virgins were captured in Cologne by Huns who demanded that they should renounce Christianity; they refused and were put to death. In the paintings that relate the tale, St Ursula is depicted wearing blue and white garments similar to those that frequently identify the Virgin Mary. Particularly valuable topographically are Memling's views of medieval Cologne, a city that he knew well.

The Triptychs

Centrally placed in front of the altar is the large *St John the Baptist and St John the Evangelist* triptych, painted specifically for the high altar of the chapel in 1479. It is generally referred to as the St John altarpiece, but occasionally as the Mystic Marriage of St Catherine, due to the central panel, in which the infant Christ is depicted presenting St Catherine with a ring. It has been suggested that Memling modelled his portrait of the saint on Mary of Burgundy. Also featured are St John the Baptist and St John the Evangelist, patron saints of the hospital; the fronts of the side panels illustrate scenes from their lives, whilst the backs depict the four donors of the triptych kneeling before their patron saints.

Displayed against the south wall is a much smaller triptych, commissioned for the hospital by another of its brothers, Jan Floreins, in 1479, and known as the *Adoration of the Magi* triptych. The 36-year-old Floreins is shown kneeling to the left of the central panel. Left of the Virgin, the king may be a portrait of Charles the Bold.

Yet a third but less impressive triptych, *Lamentations over Christ*, is seen next. It was commissioned from Memling in 1480 by another brother of the hospital, Adriaan Reins, and is based on a work by Rogier van der Weyden at whose studio in Brussels Memling had learnt his craft before coming to Bruges. Reins, the donor, kneels in the left panel. In spite of its emotional subject, the central panel fails to move. Painted on the right panel is an appealing St Barbara.

In the subsidiary north chapel of Sint Cornelius, added in the fifteenth century,are two works transferred here from the St Juliaanshospitaal in south Bruges, which closed in 1815. The first seen, *Sibylla Sambetha*, is a mysterious portrait believed to depict the daughter of Willem Moreel, Burgemeester of Bruges in 1480, when the work was painted. Inscribed at the top left corner of the Renaissance-period frame of the painting is the name Sibylla Sambetha, a Persian whose prophecy of Christ's coming is quoted below. It is not known who was responsible for this or why the title was chosen, but the name has stuck, due to the ethereal expression of the young lady.

The last work, the **Nieuwen-hove diptych**, is a rare example of a medieval diptych that remains undivided. Painted in 1487, the young donor and subject of one of the two panels, Martin van Nieuwenhove, was only 23 years old at the time. Exit from the hospital left and pass through the archway, left.

Immediately right, approached from a cloister passageway, the seventeenth-century **pharmacy** of the hospital only ceased to operate in 1973. Items such as bottles, wooden dressers and splendid examples of Delftware jars are seen, many in their original position.

In the rear room, a cupboard is carved with a bas-relief depicting a hospital ward in which patients, can be seen two to a bed: one trusts that modern welfare state economies will not have to repeat such drastic measures! In addition to sick patients impecunious travellers were also accommodated in the hospital, many of whom would have been used to sharing a bed with a stranger. The hospital possesses an even better record of the ward's appearance, as revealed in an eighteenth century painting near the entrance by Jan Beerblock. Beds are shown created in alcoves, patients transported on wooden litters and dogs frisk without hinderance.

From Sint Janshospitaal, Mariastraat continues southward, merging with Katelijnestraat, an important but not particularly interesting shopping street. However, recently opened at 43 Katelijnestraat is the **Diamont Museum**.

Nieuwe Gentweg, second left, possesses one of the longest unbroken stretches of almshouses in Bruges, where two establishments, **Godshuis Sint Jozef** (1674) and **Godshuis Meulenaere** (1613). merge between numbers eight and twenty-four. The beautifully maintained courtyard garden of the latter may be entered from the splendid Baroque portal. Much of the charm of Bruges is created by its ancient almshouses, originally built by philanthropic citizens to provide basic accommodation for the destitute. There are still fifty in existence, all now modernized internally and managed by the state.

Further along the street at number 53 is **De Snippe**, a hotel/restaurant which, although unprepossessing externally, serves some of the finest cuisine in Bruges, concentrating on French specialities, particularly fish. Its restaurant is a delight, with delicate murals and splendid chandeliers of Murano glass.

A return westward leads to Drie Kroezenstraat, left, where at its south end, the seven gables of **Godshuis Onze-Lieve-Vrouwe der Zeven Ween** (Almshouse of the Virgin of the Seven Sorrows) were the inspiration for its name. On the Baroque portal is inscribed the date 1654.

Oude Gentweg, right, leads to Katelijnestraat, right, from where Walstraat, first left, continues to the always lively **Walplein**.

Walplein's bars

A rectangular-shaped square, Walplein is almost entirely devoted to tourist bars and restaurants. **De Zevende Hemel** (Seventh Heaven) restaurant occupies an ancient, step-gabled house. Directly opposite, nestling beneath the trees, the bronze group is entitled *Leda, Pegasus, Prometheus and Zeus*, but there was no sign of Zeus at the time of writing – perhaps he was having a quick drink in one of the adjacent bars!

And a brewery

On the opposite side of the square is one of the few breweries still functioning in Bruges, **De Halve Maan** (Half Moon). This trademark derived from the name of the Bruges house that brewer Henri Maes first occupied in 1564. Incidentally, by tradition, the first son born to each generation of the Maes family is always called Henri. Visits may be made to the brewery at the rear, which was founded here in 1856 to produce Straffe Hendrik, a speciality beer with a very pronounced flavour – as may be expected, tastings are included in the admission price.

Vast quantities of Straffe Hendrik beer are available throughout Belgium; most of it, however, comes from a modern, much larger brewery located elsewhere in West Flanders.

Wijngaardstraat

From the south end of Walplein, Wijngaardstraat, right, leads to the bridge that faces the Begijnhof. Although short, Wijngaardstraat has a wide selection of restaurants, some of them offering reasonably-priced table d'hôte menus, not easily found elsewhere in Bruges.

A short detour

Before continuing ahead to the Begijnhof, a short detour southward along Noordstraat (virtually a continuation of Walplein) leads to an exceptionally picturesque group of alms-houses, **Het Godshuis De Vos**, built around an open courtyard in 1713 and immaculately restored in 1995; its tiny, private chapel has survived.

Ahead, on the Arsenaalstraat corner of Noordstraat, rises an enormous **medieval chimney** with a vaulted cooking recess. The structure is a sixteenth-century remnant (with twentieth-century buttresses) of the former Bogarden Convent that once stood here. It now lies on the fringe of the nineteenth-century complex of buildings housing the **Academy of Fine Arts**, formerly located in the Poortersloge in what is still called Academiestraat.

On returning to Wijngaardstraat, take the right fork at its west end and cross the bridge to the pedimented

Diamant Museum (see p.48)

Classical gateway of the **Begijnhof**, (or Beguinage, its French name) dated 1776 and restored in 1995. Within a niche there stands a figure of St Elizabeth of Hungary, patron of the foundation.

Begijnhof

After the belfry and the town hall, the **Begijnhof** is the best-known location in Bruges. It resembles a large almshouse, with small dwellings and a church surrounding a tree-studded green.

History

As was to reoccur after World War I, unspeakable carnage during the wars of the Crusades meant that many young women in Europe were widowed, and unmarried maidens had little prospect of marriage unless they were exceptionally comely or hailed from a wealthy family. Great hardship was to ensue.

In order to care for these destitute women, Lambert le Bègue, a Liège priest, founded the charitable Order of the Beguines around 1189. Nothing survives of the first beguinage at Liège, but in the thirteenth century, two of Boudewijn of Constantinople's daughters, Margaret and Joanna, revived the concept by setting up beguinages at Ghent, Antwerp, Leuven, Kortrijk, Lier and Amsterdam.

Margaret of Constantinople, Countess of Flanders, founded the Bruges Begijnhof in approximately 1245, a century before a similar development, which also survives, was established at Amsterdam. Although not strictly monastic, the Begijnhof accommodated women who wished to follow a convent lifestyle without being fully committed to it. Some took vows of chastity, but were permitted to leave and marry if they changed their minds. They were not idle: at Bruges their tasks included lace-making or caring for children and the sick, under the direction of the *grootjuffrouw* (Great Lady).

The Begijnhof is particularly attractive in early spring, when a myriad of daffodils bloom: Winston Churchill delighted in painting this magnificent scene. At Ghent the houses of some begijnhofs are also grouped around central greens, but the other examples in Belgium are planned as a series of narrow, interconnecting streets.

Begijnhof Museum

Immediately after entering the complex, house number C1, to the left may be visited. Once a begijn's dwelling, it now serves as a small museum (closed 12noon–3.45pm) in which is displayed

Wijngaardstraat's restaurants are reasonably priced

a painting of the annual sacrement procession in the Begijnhof. No begijns have lived here since 1930, when the last died, and they were replaced by the present occupants, sisters of the Benedictine Order, whose members continue to live here and still wear fifteenth-century habits.

The approach to the Begijnhof, it may be recalled, was made from Wijngardstraat (Vineyard Street), and the official name of the establishment is Prinselijk Begijnhof ten Wijngaarde (Princely Begijnhof of the Vineyard). 'Princely' refers to the adoption of the

Order in 1299 by the King of France, Philip the Fair, but 'vineyard' puzzles many. The explanation is that the site was a *meer*, Dutch for marsh, which the French mistranslated as vineyard; one assumes that the marsh was drained soon after the begijns settled there.

Begijnhof church

A pathway, from which each house and the church may be reached, encircles the green. The **Begijnhof church**, dedicated to St Elizabeth of Hungary, stands on the east side, its chancel facing the water. Founded in Burg as the chapel of the heir to the Count of Flanders, Margaret of Constantinople, Countess of Flanders, transferred its parish in 1245 to the newly-built Begijnhof. The earlier church was badly damaged by fire in 1584 and rebuilt in 1602.

St Elizabeth, depicted in a niche above the entrance, is also the subject of the most important work within the church, the altar painting by Jacob van

The Sashuis (sluice house), Minnewater

Oost the Elder. An amusing and apparently truthful story refers to the book in the painting, which was added during restoration work in 1802 as replacement for a dog. The Grand Lady, it appears, decided that the animal, although small, was an undignified companion for the begijns' patron saint, and ordered the amendment.

The choir screen incorporates a piece of stone cut from the rock at Lourdes where the Virgin Mary is alleged to have made an appearance.

Begijnhof's houses

It will be noted that the houses, most of which date from the seventeenth and eighteenth centuries, vary in design, partly because all the originals have been replaced at different times. The Gothic style, however, has been maintained; C4, for example, exhibits pointed arches and foiled tracery, even though it was built in the seventeenth century. All, however, are whitewashed and retain wrought-iron bell pulls. One house, considerably larger than the others (number 30 on the south side), was the residence of the Grand Lady.

Minnewater

A return through the main gateway of the Begijnhof and a right turn after the bridge has been crossed leads to romantic Minnewater, a lake created around 1200 to form a harbour for craft using the Lieve Canal to Ghent. Sluices near the present Sashuis (sluice house) probably formed the first barrier. Views, which are extremely romantic in any case, are enhanced by swans gliding sedately on the waters. However, it is certain that Minnewater does not mean 'Lake of Love', as is popularly supposed. A more likely translation is Inner Harbour, but it has been suggested that *minne* referred to a boat turning round to leave the harbour.

To explore Minnewater, follow the path on the west side towards the bridge. Adjoining **Minnewaterpark**, located on the east side of the lake, is a nineteenth century mock-Gothic castle, now a top class restaurant, Kasteel Minnewater. The park and restaurant can both be reached from Arsenaalstraat.

Twin towers were built by Jan van Oudenaarde for defensive purposes around 1400, at the south end of the rectangular lake, which interrupted the city wall at this point. One of the towers survives in its entirety, **Poertoren** (Powder Tower), built in 1398, and so named because gunpowder and weapons were stored within it. Most of the other tower, constructed three years later, was demolished around 1621; however its base, which still exists, served as an ice house from 1780 to 1914.

The bridge was constructed in 1740, originally with an unobstructed central span to permit the passage of high vessels, in particular a barge that was towed by horses regularly between Bruges and Ghent. The central arch is, therefore, a later addition.

Some weary visitors may now be relieved to hear that this lengthy excursion is now almost at an end, the railway/bus station only being a few minutes' walk away. This is reached by turning right at the Poertoren and following Begijnvest westward. At its end turn left and continue ahead to Stationsplein, where there are local buses and expensive taxis.

Places to Visit

The Belfry Interior

7 Markt
Open: 1 Apr to 30 Sept 9.30am–5pm;
1 Oct to 31 Mar 9.30am–12.30pm,
1.30–5pm.
Admission charge

Heilig Bloed Basiliek

(Holy Blood Basilica)
13 Burg
Open: 1 Apr to 30 Sept 9.30am–12noon,
2–6pm; 1 Oct to 31 Mar 10am–12noon,
2–4pm.
Admission free

Provinciaal Museum Het Brugse Vrije

11a Burg
Open: 1 Apr to 30 Sept 9.30am–12.30pm,
1.15–5pm; 1 Oct to 31 Mar 9.30am–
12.30pm, 2–5pm.

Groeninge Museum

12 Dijver
Open: 1 Apr to 30 Sept 9.30am–5pm. 1
Oct to 31 Mar 9.30am–12.30pm, 2–5pm.
Closed Tue.
Admission charge

Arentshuismuseum

16 Dijver
Open: 1 Apr to 30 Sept 9.30am–5pm. 1
Oct to 31 Mar 9.30am–12.30pm, 2–5pm.
Closed Tue.
Lace display and Brangwyn Collection
Admission charge

Onze-Lieve-Vrouwekerk

O-L-V Kerkhof Zuid Chancel
Mon to Fri 9am–12.30pm, 1.30pm—5pm,
Sun 1.30pm–5pm, Sat 9am–12.30pm,
1.30pm–4pm.

Gruuthuse Museum

17 Dijver
Open: 1 Apr to 30 Sept 9.30am–5pm. 1
Oct to 31 Mar 9.30am–12.30pm, 2–5pm.
Closed Tue.
Admission charge

Sint Janshospitaal

38 Mariastraat
Open: 1 Apr to 30 Sept 9.30am–5pm. 1
Oct to 31 Mar 9.30am–12.30pm, 2–5pm.
Closed Wed.
Admission charge.

Diamant Museum

45 Katelijnestraat
www.diamondmuseum.be
Open: daily 10.30am–5.30pm. Polishing
at 12.25pm. Admission charge. No free
samples unfortunately!

Straffe Hendrik

26 Walplein
☎ 050 332697
Open: 1 Apr to 30 Sept 10am–5pm
(continuously).
Open: 1 Oct to 31 Mar 11am and 3pm.
Brewery Tour. Admission charge. Groups
on request

Straffe Hendrik

26 Walplein
Open: 1 May to 30 Sept, Wed to Sun
2–5pm.
Brewery Museum

Begijnhof

Open: Dec, Jan and Feb. Mon and Fri
11am–12noon. Wed 11am–12noon,
2–4pm. Thur 2–4pm. 1 Mar to 30 Nov,
daily, 10am–12noon, 1.45pm–5pm (5.30
Sat and Sun, 1 Apr to 30 Sept).
Admission free (except museum).

2. North-East Bruges

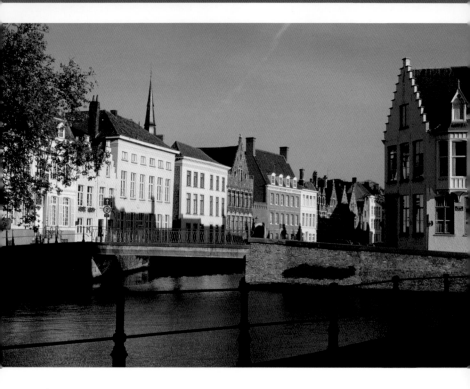

Route 2

Starting and ending at Markt, this itinerary includes some of the finest churches in Bruges, most of them with Gothic exteriors and Baroque interiors.

Churches, museums & windmills

Not to be missed are the O-L-V Pot-terie Hospital and the premises of the St Sebastian's Guild, in which are displayed several items demonstrating the guild's close ties with British monarchs. The route followed, which will be much less crowded with tourists than the previous route, may be completed in half a day – as long as not too much time is spent in the brewery and taverns passed on route.

From the north end of **Markt** follow Philipstockstraat eastward. On the left, 1 Keerstraat, is the church known as **Het Keerske**. Founded in 1080 as the double chapel of the Chandlers Guild (hence its name, which means the Candle), dedicated to St Peter and St Katherine, it was entirely rebuilt in 1725 and heavily restored in 1987. Whilst the interior is of no greater architectural interest than the exterior, some English visitors may wish to enter, as it is here that Church of England services in Bruges are held every Sunday at 6pm. When Burg is reached, cross between the trees to the south side and the bridged **Blinde Ezelstraat** (see box below).

Virgin of Ourdenaarde

Before proceeding beneath the arch into Blinde Ezelstraat, note, immediately right on the facade of **Stadhuis**, a carved figure of the Virgin of Ourdenaarde. She holds an inkwell as did both earlier statues of her, and was adopted as their patron by the Clerical Guild. In order to protect the rather exposed figure, a cage was fixed around it, as can be seen from contemporary paintings of Burg. This expediency, however, failed to save the carving from French revolutionary iconoclasts and, like the other examples, this piece of sculpture is recent work.

At the end of Blinde Ezelstraat, a right turn leads to one of the city's most photogenic quarters.

Blinde Ezelstraat

The strange name of this street, meaning Blind Donkey, is said to be a reference to an eponymous tavern owned by the bishop, which once stood in the narrow thoroughfare. Apparently, the cheapest beer in the city was served within, and many patrons became 'blind donkeys', an expression for drunkards. A rather nastier story about the derivation of the street's name, almost certainly untrue, is told of a trader's donkey that repeatedly refused to go down the street because something he saw there frightened him; to overcome this, the owner blinded the poor creature.

Huidenvettersplein

In this small square, artists may be seen, some of them occasionally working on their 'masterpieces', and the scene resembles a miniature version of Place du Tertre in the Montmartre quarter of Paris.

The buildings of greatest interest line the west side, all of them backing the canal, and all of them possessing restaurants. **Hotel Duc de Bourgogne**, built in 1648, has two stepped gables. Huidenvettershuis, dated 1630, is castellated and now forms part of **'t Dreveken** restaurant, the first section of which dates from the rebuilding of 1664. This was originally the guildhouse of the huidenvetters (tanners), and aspects of their trade are depicted in the bas-reliefs of the facade. Restaurant specialities include rabbit with prunes, and chicken in a casserole with beer.

From the south side of the square, more steps descending to the waterside indicate another staging point for boat trips. Ahead, the view across the water to the belfry from Rozenhoedkaai, the most famous in Bruges, was painted by Winston Churchill.

Rozenhoedkaai

Rozenhoedkaai (Rosary Quay) refers to the rosaries' beads of ivory and amber that were once sold here to devout Catholics. Rainer Maria Rilke (1874–1965) referred in the title of his book *Quai de Rosaire* to the quay. In earlier times, the thoroughfare was called Zoutkaai (Salt Quay), as great quantities of salt from France and Germany were unloaded there.

From Rozenhoedkaai it may be observed that the rear of Huidenvettershuis is step-gabled, rather than castellated like its front. At the Nepomucenus Bridge end of the quay, above seven windows of the first house on the south side, lunettes are carved with bas-reliefs depicting the Seven Acts of Mercy.

Pandreitje

Follow Pandreitje, which continues southward from Huidenvettersplein, passing the west side of a small park, the splendid trees of which frame views of the belfry. Perhaps only a few will wish to continue southward to observe the monumental nineteenth century gateway, all that survives of the state prison of Pandreitje. The remainder of the large site has been redeveloped.

The name Pand (in Pandreitje), meaning Pawn, derives from the stand of the jewellers and goldsmiths that was erected annually for the Bruges spring fair on part of the future site of the prison until, in 1671, a house of correction, primarily for vagabonds, was built. On conversion to a state prison in 1827, the adjacent **Vleeshuis** (Meathouse) of the master butchers was incorporated, and most of the complex rebuilt; the **gatehouse** dates from this period.

Pandreitje (the street) leads to Gevangenisstraat, followed by the street simply called Park, as it overlooks **Koningin Astrid Park**, the former grounds of a Franciscan monastery, now the most popular open space in the city centre. Its name commemorates the much loved Swedish-born Queen Astrid, consort of King Leopold III. During a visit to Switzerland in 1935, the King was driving his car when it crashed, killing

Astrid. Heavy mourning throughout Belgium followed, many blaming the unfortunate Leopold for the tragedy. The Queen's statue may be seen at the north-west end of the enclosure. Parallels with the tragic car accident in which Diana, Princess of Wales, died in 1997 have been noted.

L'Estaminet, one of the most attractive bars in Bruges, stands on the north side of the park Beamed ceilings and hops give a venerable appearance to the interior, which is rare in Bruges. The bar is shut all day Thursday, and Monday after 2pm.

From the north-west corner of the park, Jozef Suveestraat leads northward to Vismarkt (see box above). Those who have not visited Koningin Astrid Park may reach it by returning eastward along Rozenhoedkaai to Braambergstraat, which skirts its south side.

Braambergstraat continues eastward from the south end of Vismarkt. At number 7, the former trading house of the Fishporters, built in 1637, has been converted to a wine bar. Return to Vismarkt.

Brugse Vrije's 15th century gables

The east side of Vismarkt leads northwards to Steenhouwersdijk, from where there are splendid views across the canal to the Gothic gables of the **Brugse Vrije**, which were spared when the range facing Burg was rebuilt in the eighteenth century. It is pleasant to follow the canal eastward to where the street becomes Groenerei and curves sharply southward.

Best viewed from Peerdenbrug (the

> # Vismarkt
>
> Vismarkt (Fish Market) comprises stalls grouped permanently around a central courtyard in which stands an enormous water pump. Tuscan colonnades support roofs that give some protection from the weather. The complex was built in Empire style by the municipal architect in 1821, and is the only public development of importance in Bruges dating from the brief period when Belgium and Holland were reunited (1815–30). The Bruges fish market had occupied part of the north side of Markt until 1745. The market operates 6am to 1pm but not on Sunday or Monday. Wednesday and Friday mornings are the liveliest times to visit; little is left by midday. As may be expected, there are several bars and fish restaurants grouped around Vismarkt.

bridge ahead) are the five linked almshouses at 8–12 Groenerei, each with its dormer window, that comprise **Godshuis de Pelikaan**, founded in 1634. Look for the relief above a doorway of a pelican feeding its young with its own blood (a Christian symbol of charity).

At Predikherenbrug, the canal leading southward is known as **Coupure**. It was excavated in the mid-eighteenth century, and flows towards the river in a straight line for ease of navigation. This stretch now provides moorings for pleasure craft.

Cross the bridge, left Langestraat, first right Molenmeers. In Verbrand Nieuwland, first right, visitors may enter the gate at number 10 for guided tours of **De Gouden Boom Brewery** and/or

Route 2

0 50 100 150 200 250 metres
0 50 100 150 200 250 yards

N
W — E
S

Portinsrei
Duinenbrug
Leeuwenberg
Oognodossa
Potterstraat
Oliebaan
Gotje
Langerei
Snaggaardstr.
St Gillis Kerkhof
Snaggaardbrug
St Gilliskoorstr.
St Gillis Kerkstr.
Carmersstr.
Rolweg
Kruisstr.
Gouden Handbrug
Handstr.
Gouden
Carmersbrug
Carmersstr.
Korte Ropeerdstr.
Blekersstr.
Strobrug
St Anna
Jeruzalemstr.
Stijn Streuvelsstr.
Peperstr.
Langestr.
Spiegelrei
Spinolarei
St Annaplein
Verversdijk
Rodestr.
De Nieuwe Beos
Molenaers
Jan Van Eyckplein
St Maartensplein
Boomgaardstr.
Verbrand Nieuwland
Molenbrug
Philipstockstr.
Hoogstr.
Langestr.
Predikherenbrug
Markt
Burg
Blindstr.
Breidelstr.
Steenhouwersdijk
Peterkenbrug
Greinere
Predikherenstr.
Coupure
Huidenvetterspl.
Braamberstr.
Park
Nieuwstraat koning
Koningin Astridpark
P

1 ● 2 ● 3 ● 4 ● 5 ● 6 ● 7 ● 8 ● 9 ● 10 ● 11 ● 12 ● 13 ● 14 ● 15 ● 16 ● 17 ● 18 ● 19 ● 20 ● 21 ● 22 ● 23 ● 24 ●

The Hotel Duc de Bourgogne,
Huidenvettershuis and 't Dreveken
restaurant, seen from Rozenhoedkaai

KEY — Route 2

1. Het Keerske (The Anglican Church)
2. Rozenhoedkaai
3. Vismarkt (Fish Market)
4. Godshuis de Pelikaan (almshouses)
5. De Gouden Boom
   (Brewery and Malthouse Museum)
6. Sint Annakerk (St Anne's Church)
7. Jeruzalemkerk (Jerusalem Church)
8. Kantcentrum (Lace Centre)
9. Museum voor Volkskunde
   (Folklore Museum)
10. Kruispoort (City gate)
11. Bonne Chiere (windmill)
12. Sint Jorisgilde (St George's Guild)

     Walking route

13. Guido Gezellemuseum
14. Engels Klooster (The English Convent)
15. Sint Sebastiaansgilde
    (St Sebastian's Guild)
16. Sint Janshuysmolen
    (windmill, operates in summer)
17. De Nieuwe Papegaai (windmill)
18. De Coeleweymolen (windmill)
19. Onze-Lieve-Vrouw ter Potterie
    (Our Lady of the Pottery Museum)
20. Bisschoppelijk Seminarie
    (Episcopal Seminary)
21. Duinenbrug (wooden bridge)
22. Sint Gilliskerk (St Giles Church)
23. Vlissinghe (ancient tavern)
24. Sint Walburgakerk (St Walburga's Church)

visits to its museum (see below).

From the brewery, return to Molen-meers, turn right and take the second turning left, Joost de Damhouderstraat, to Sint Annaplein.

Sint Annakerk

Within Sint Annaplein stands Sint Annakerk (St Anne's Church), a 1624 rebuilding of an earlier church, founded in 1497 but completely destroyed by iconoclasts in 1586 during the period of religious strife.

Externally, the brick building is basically an undemonstrative example of the late-Gothic style; however, it can be seen that the windows of the nave were originally larger.

On entering Sint Annakerk (May–September only) it is immediately revealed that the interior is Baroque rather than the expected Gothic. With its dark oak, chancel screen and brass

De Gouden Boom Brewery

The brewery was established in 1587, but its present buildings date from the early years of the twentieth century. Brewed here are Abdij Steenbrugge, Brugs Tarbier, a wheat beer sometimes drunk with a slice of lemon, and the very strong Brugse Tripel (9.5 per cent) with a rather sweet flavour.

The museum is located in the former Malthouse of 1902; exhibits include brewing machinery, barrels, bottles, ancient documents and a reconstructed Bruges café of around 1900. Visitors to the brewery itself are shown the entire brewing process from grain delivery to the final product. All are given a glass of beer.

chandeliers, the interior evokes one of Sir Christopher Wren's more ambitious City of London churches. Flemish carving had reached its high point when the church was built, and there are masterly examples throughout. Unusually exuberant is the woodwork of the nave, with its range of barley sugar pilasters. The pulpit, confessionals and stalls are all crisply carved, but it is perhaps the marble rood screen between the nave and the chancel that most takes the eye, with its gleaming brass mounts.

Above the exit, at the west end, the Last Judgement mural was painted by Herregoudts in 1685.

From the rear of Sint Annakerk, Jeruzalemstraat, right, stretches eastward to Peperstraat on the corner of which stands the most eccentric church in Bruges, little-altered since it was built.

Jeruzalemkerk

Jeruzalemkerk (Jerusalem Church) was founded around 1427 by Pieter and Jacob Adornes, descendants of a thirteenth-century Genoese merchant who had settled in Bruges after taking part in the crusades. It was built for the private use of the Adornes family. Anselm Adornes, the son of Pieter, visited Jerusalem from which he returned with relics, many of which survive in the building.

Entered from the south side, the church consists of three separate chapels, two of them on the ground floor, the third occupying the high-ceilinged upper storey. By tradition, Jeruzalemkerk was modelled on the Church of the Holy Sepulchre in Jerusalem, which the crusading Anselms would have seen, and this is the reason for its name. Most

are surprised by the compactness of the building, which only becomes apparent after it has been entered.

The unusually low, black marble tombchest of Anselm Adornes and his wife Margarethe, surmounted by their recumbent figures, stands in the **entrance chapel**; Gothic lettering on the sides is now hard to decipher. Anselm Adornes, who served as a diplomat for the Duke of Burgundy, was asked by King James III of Scotland to look after the interests of Scottish wool traders in Flanders. During a visit to Scotland, Adornes was murdered on 23 January 1483 and buried in Linlithgow Palace. All that lies in Anselm's tomb-chest is his heart, which was brought to Bruges.

Stained glass windows, dated 1432, and wall monuments commemorate members of the family, which still owns the church. The Adornes emblem of a wheel and a halo will be noted.

In the small **side chapel** is displayed a model of Jerusalem's Holy Sepulchre, incorporating a figure of Christ, and a gilded reliquary said to contain a fragment of the Holy Cross.

The **upper chapel**, reached by the steps, may be viewed but not entered; its ceiling is surprisingly high for such a small area. If the church's main door is locked, a side door by the Lace Centre entrance usually gives access. There is a small charge, which covers entrance to the Church and Lace Centre, including the demonstration.

Kantcentrum

Next to Jeruzalemkerk, in Peperstraat, the Adornes family founded an almshouse which has been converted to the **Kantcentrum** (Lace Centre). Every afternoon except Sunday, approximately twenty women of various ages can be observed making bobbin lace; the intricate but confident movement of their hands can be quite hypnotic. Articles are sold, and unidentified examples of lacework displayed.

Return to Jeruzalemkerk and follow Balstraat northward, passing, right, the Junior Lace School at number 14, to the Rolweg corner, left.

Museum Voor Volkskunde

The **Museum Voor Volkskunde** (Folklore Museum) occupies a group of rooms in what was formerly the Shoemakers' almshouse. Each is fitted out to represent an ancient Bruges shop or living area. Of particular interest are: **room 3** with its splendid display of copper moulds for use in the kitchen, the apothecary in **room 4**, and the collection of pipes in **room 14**.

The ancient Kruispoort gateway

Four locations of only marginal interest lie to the east, but those with sufficient time at their disposal may wish to see them. A return to Peperstraat, passing the Kantcentrum and following the street to its end, brings the visitor to **Kruispoort**. one of the ancient gateways of Bruges.

First erected in 1402 at the same time as Gentpoort, another gate that also survives to the south, Kruispoort was built of white sandstone rather than the usual brick; much rebuilding has taken place, and the gate was restored in 1972. All the gates of Bruges punctuated the defensive wall that was constructed on the city side of the river in the thirteenth and fourteenth centuries.

Kruisvest follows the river-bank northward passing, right, the **Bonne Chiere Windmill**. Originally constructed in East Flanders in 1888, this windmill was re-erected on the Bruges rampart in 1911 for picturesque reasons, and not restored to working order.

The windmill faces Stijn Streuvelsstraat, where on the right, a modern building accommodates a fourteenth-century foundation: the **Sint Jorisgilde**.

Sint Jorisgilde

Accommodated since 1958 in a modern building, at 59 Stijn Streuvelsstraat is the **Sint Jorisgilde** (Guild of St George). Founded in 1321, this was one of the medieval guilds of crossbow archers that protected the city. King Charles II of England made a donation to the guild during his exile in Bruges following the Civil War.

If a member is present, it may be possible to see the guild's Golden Book containing the signatures of the kings of Belgium and visiting heads of state.

In the **Shooting Room** is a magnificent collection of ancient crossbows. The guild's most important painting hangs behind the top table in the **Council Hall**; it depicts Albert Casimir of Austria, Prince of Poland, and Maria Christina, Princess of Hungary and Bohemia.

The original guildhouse, now a school, survives some distance away at 5 Hugo Losschaertstraat, off Sint Jorisstraat, which is a continuation northward of Vlamingstraat.

Exit from Sint Jorisgilde left, first left

Jeruzalemkerk & Kantcentrum (Lace Centre)

Kruisvest, second left Rolweg and the **Guido Gezellemuseum** (of limited interest to non Dutch-speaking visitors).

Guido Gezellemuseum

Guido Gezelle, Belgium's most famous lyric poet, was born in this house in 1830, coincidentally the year in which his country gained its independence. By 1854, he was teaching at a school in Roeselare, West Flanders, and was ordained a priest the same year. Almost immediately, Gezelle began to write poetry, much of it a paean to the beauty of nature, which, apart from the love of God, was to be his greatest inspiration.

It appears that the young priest found the attractions of his nubile pupils difficult to resist, and he was quietly transferred from Roeselare to Bruges in 1860 to serve as vice-principal and professor of philosophy to a recently founded Anglo/Belgian seminary. Gezelle was very much an anglophile, speaking English perfectly. He served as assistant priest at Sint Walburgakerk (1865–1872) and founded a literary magazine. Un-

Undoubtedley the most famous view in Bruges: the Belfry from Rozenhoedkaai

Gothic spires and turrets decorate the 15th century facade of Brugse Vrije

willing to moderate his non-liberal views, Gezelle met with strong opposition; dispirited, his health began to fail and he moved to Kortrijk to serve as a chaplain. Fortunately, Gezelle's translation of Longfellow's epic poem *The Song of Hiawatha* into Dutch revived both his popularity and his health.

In the spring of 1899, Guido Gezelle returned once more to Bruges, having been appointed chaplain of the Engels Klooster (English Convent). During a brief visit to England the same year, Gezelle caught an infection from which he died on 27 November 1899, shortly after his return to Bruges.

In 1926, three rooms in Gezelle's birthplace were converted to a museum, where memorabilia and various editions of the poet's work may be seen; some poems have been translated into English. On display is the pipe that Gezelle was extremely fond of smoking; by tradition, it broke the day before he died. A bust

Bonne Chiere windmill

of Gezelle may be seen to the rear in the pleasant garden.

A perambulation westward along **Rolweg** leads to the **Museum voor Volkskunde**, from where those who have not taken the diversion, as well as those who have, may proceed northward, following Korte Speelmansstraat to Carmersstraat, first right.

Street corner shrines

At the junction, fitted in a niche in the building on the north-east corner, is a wooden **Virgin and Child statue**, carved in the eighteenth century and one of the finest of around 500 religious figures that are still to be seen in the streets of Bruges.

Turn right along Carmersstraat, the name of which records the thirteenth-century Carmelite Convent that stood there for five hundred years on the site of the present St Leo College (Potterierei). It was pulled down in 1584, rebuilt in the seventeenth century, and finally demolished in 1796.

Follow Carmersstraat eastward.

Located in Carmersstraat, this Virgin & Child figure is regarded as one of the finest in the city

Engels Klooster

Defined by its domed church, the Engels Klooster (English Convent) dominates the north side of the street.

Since the reign of Queen Elizabeth I, life had been difficult for Catholics in England, and those who wished to lead a monastic existence had to leave the country; many fled to the continent. The convent of St Ursula at Leuven accepted novice nuns from England, who would later found their own Augustinian convent. In 1629, several hundred of them duly transferred to Bruges, occupying a large building called Nazareth. Catherine of Braganza, the Portuguese-born consort of England's Charles II and still a Catholic, presented the English Convent with her rosary and some valuable specimens of lace.

The convent's first chapel was built here in 1650. Six years prior to this, Henry More the great-grandson of Sir Thomas More who had been executed by Henry VIII, was appointed visiting priest. Remaining in the possession of the Engels Klooster is a relic of Sir Thomas, which Henry presented to them. After Sir Thomas More's execution, his body is believed to have been interred in the Tower of London, but his head was kept by Margaret Roper, his daughter, at her house in Eltham; after her death, this was buried at St Dunstan, Canterbury. However, it appears that one of More's vertebrae was retained by his family as a relic, and it was this that Henry More donated to the sisters.

The present church was built in 1739 by the most Baroque of Bruges architects, Hendrik Pulinx; it is a rare Bruges example of a domed building.

As will be appreciated, the nuns had to flee Bruges during the French Revolution, most of them this time making their way to England, a country that by now had become much more tolerant of religious beliefs. Most returned in 1802, however, when Napoleon established religious freedom throughout his empire. Their convent, still known as Nazareth, had been sold in 1797, but the nuns were able to negotiate its return. English girls from wealthy Catholic families soon arrived to attend boarding school at the convent, and in 1887 a sister establishment was founded at Hampstead Heath, north London (this did not become autonomous until 1924). Guido Gezelle, rector for just seven months, died at the Engels Klooster in 1899. It is said that his last words were *"I loved so much to hear the birds sing"*.

Visitors are conducted to the chancel via a cloister, which was rebuilt in 1960 as a reproduction of the 1640 original. Apparently the cupola was specified for acoustic reasons; its painting depicts the Apotheosis of St Augustine.

Sint Sebastiaansgilde

Those who did not visit the Sint Joris-gilde, and those who did but were disappointed, should not neglect to continue eastward to the **Sint Sebas-tiaansgilde** at 174 Carmersstraat, accommodated in one of the most picturesque Gothic buildings in Bruges. Another medieval archers foundation – this time longbow archers – the Sint Sebastiaansgilde (Guild of St Sebastian), founded in the fourteenth century, has occupied these premises since 1573. The guild played an important part in the Crusades, and for that reason the Cross of Jerusalem is incorporated in its arms.

The building has been referred to as the 'Cradle of the Grenadier Guards', as it was here that England's Charles II founded that regiment in 1656 while still exiled in Bruges. The King himself participated in archery contests, which took place in the grounds in fine weather, or within the long gallery during the winter months. Guild members, restricted to 100, now meet primarily for social events, but many still practise their archery and participate in contests; every British sovereign since Charles II has been a member.

A beautifully proportioned outagonal tower, with an attached circular stairwell, rises beside the main, step-gabled building. Personal audio commentaries available in several languages fully describe the history of the guild and its possessions. The **Banqueting Hall** is of greatest interest, pride of place amongst the treasures displayed being given to the marble bust of Charles II, sculpted by Francois-Christophe Dieussart in 1666. During their visit in 1863, Queen Victoria and Prince Albert presented the guild with a silver cup, which is always on display. In more recent times, Queen Elizabeth II and the Duke of Edinburgh maintained the tradition of United Kingdom sovereigns presenting souvenirs of their visits to the guild. Since the time of Charles II, six kings and queens have signed the guild's visitors book.

Windmills

Sint Janshuysmolen

Carmersstraat joins Kruisvest a short distance to the east and, immediately right, perched on the grass-covered rampart, is **Sint Janshuysmolen**. This stilt windmill was built to replace an earlier version on the same site, which blew down in 1744. Sint Janshuysmolen ceased operation in 1914, but was restored to working order in 1964.

A miller, employed by the Bruges municipal authority, operates the windmill in the season – but a minimum force three to four wind is needed to set the sails in motion. Bear in mind that the wooden steps to the entrance are very steep and not suitable for young children or the infirm.

From the rampart looking southward may be seen the non-operational mill, Bonne Chiere, already referred to. It is in fact possible to take a photograph that incorporates both mills from the green facing Carmersstraat.

North from the Carmersstraat junction, the road becomes Peterseliestraat, a fairly lengthy stretch. Windmill addicts may wish to turn right at Leestenburg, continuing to Oostproostse ahead, behind which, again on the rampart, stands De Nieuwe Papegaai windmill, brought to Bruges in 1970 but not in working order. In 1966, a fourth windmill Coeleweymolen, was added to the north. Brought from Meulebeke it is open in the summer. Peterseliestraat terminates at Potterierei.

Medieval hospice

Onze-Lieve-Vrouw ter Potterie

Immediately left, overlooking the canal, is one of the city's best known attractions – **Onze-Lieve-Vrouw ter Potterie** (Our Lady of the Pottery), a medieval hospice for elderly ladies. Facing the canal are **seven dwellings** built for them; each is gabled, thus earning the foundation its name The Seven Gifts of the Holy Spirit. These are followed by the three much higher gables of the museum: the former **ward** of the hospice, built in 1529; the hospital **church** of 1359; and the **Lady Chapel**, added to the church as a south aisle in 1625.

Records suggest that the hospice was established some time before 1276, but neither the precise date nor the name of the founder are known. It is certain, however, that an ancient pottery formerly occupied the site, which is the reason, of course, for the hospital's strange name. In 1289, permission was given to build a church, no trace of which has survived. The foundation amalgamated around 1300 with a similar hospice in Goezeputstraat. As was usual in the medieval period, not only was accommodation provided for the sick, but for travellers as well. Apart from the three ancient buildings, the hospital is now a retirement home for men and women, run by the state. Before entering at number 79, observe the Gothic chimney of the former sick ward, which is visible from the street.

Seen first is the **entrance hall**, created by partitioning the former sick ward. Display panels trace the detailed history of the hospital in Dutch, but translations are provided on arrival. The hospital's collection of silver, paintings and sculpture is displayed throughout the hall and the **old ward**; most exhibits, however, are sixteenth or seventeenth century work, not the greatest artistic period in Bruges.

After the Lady Chapel had been added to the **church** in 1625, thus forming a south aisle, the Renaissance interior of the remainder was remodelled in Flemish Baroque style for the sake of unity. Inset on either side of the high altar are the tombs, left, of a hospice tutor, De Beer (died 1610) and his wife and, right, historian Nicolas Despars (died 1597).

Blocked arches on the north wall are a reminder that the church was originally open to the sick ward (prior, of course, to the creation of the hall). Separating the nave from the **chancel**, the rood screen is one of the most splendid in Bruges.

On the south wall of the **Lady Chapel** is a fine Madonna of the Pevelenberg carved in the fourteenth century (but painted in 1920). Another Madonna with Child, the Miraculous Statue of Our Lady of the Pottery, also fourteenth century work, stands on the marble altar.

The neo-Gothic tomb of St Idesbald, a Cistercian abbot of the nearby Ter Duinen Abbey (seen after leaving the hospital) is late nineteenth-century work.

Saint Idesbald (1110–1167), a Cistercian abbot of the foundation of Our Lady of the Dunes, lies in the tomb chest in the vestry on the south side of the Lady Chapel. The abbey was originally situated at Dunkirk but its name Ter Duinen (of the Dunes) was kept when it transferred to Bruges, south of the hospital. The present tomb of the saint is relatively modern neo-Gothic work.

From the hospital, the route follows Potterierei southward passing what, in medieval times, was the site of a shipbuilders yard.

Episcopal Seminary

In contrast to the other buildings of Potterierei, which are relatively small, the
Bisschoppelijk Seminarie (Episcopal
Seminary) at number 72, is enormous.
Built around a green, with its church at
the north end, the building originally
formed a Cistercian Abbey known as
Ter Duinen (of the Dunes – a reference to its coastal foundation). In 1834,
the buildings were taken over by the
Bishop of Bruges and the Episcopal
Seminary was installed; the present
church, built in 1788, was soon given
the present Baroque-style gable to its
canal frontage.

Permission to view the church must
be obtained from the house at the south
end of the complex, but few will find it
of great interest. The Seminary is built
around a great courtyard, and the church
is entered from the north-west corner
of its enclosed, cloistered passage, the
walls of which display large paintings,
mostly portraits. Apart from a canopied
Grecian structure behind the altar and
carved misericord stalls, the interior is
rather plain.

Immediately south of the seminary
is the picturesque **Duinenbrug** which,
although not ancient, is a rare Bruges
example of a wooden bridge that can be
raised and lowered to allow craft to pass.
Cross the next bridge, Snaggaardbrug to
Langerei, left. First right, Sint Gilliskoor-
straat provides a splendid view of Sint
Gilliskerk ahead.

Sint Gilliskerk

Sint Gilliskerk (St Giles Church) is
entered from its west end between 3pm
and 6pm only. It was begun in 1240, but
no Romanesque features appear to have
survived externally, primarily because
aisles were added between 1462 and
1479, both of them the same height as
the existing nave. The nave and chancel,
however, retain a Romanesque barrel
vault of timber, the only example in
Bruges to survive. All structural work is
of brick apart from the two piers of the
nave, which are built of stone.

The history of the Trinitarian broth-
erhood is related in four works by the
Brugean artist Jan Garemijn, which are
the only paintings of importance in the
church.

A memorial erected in 1994 commemorates the 500th anniversary of
the death of Hans Memling, the great
painter, who was buried in Sint Gilliskerk, although his grave has never
been discovered. It is also known that
the painter Lanceloot Blondeel was
buried in the church in 1561, but his
grave and tombstone have similarly
been lost. Sint Gilliskerk possesses two
organs, the oldest of them in the gallery
of the church's north aisle, and a modern
instrument in the south aisle which is
played in the organ competition that
forms part of the Flanders fair.

Van Eyck's House

Running southward from the church
is Sint Gilliskerkstraat. Left, Gouden
Handstraat where the painter, Jan van
Eyck, lived at number 6 , left. The street
leads to Gouden Handbrug, right, and is
immediately followed by Carmersbrug,
another bridge, left, at right angles to it.
Cross to Sint Annarei, first right, and
turn first left along Blekersstraat where
at number 2 is Vlissinghe tavern.

Return to Sint Annarei and cross Stro-

Vlissinghe tavern

One of the most famous taverns in Bruges, (open from noon but closed Mondays and Tuesdays) Vlissinghe is reputed to have opened as a cafe in 1515, but not under its present name. Although some of the decor is seventeenth century, a great deal of kitsch has been added recently – not to everyone's approval. Regulars still frequent the tavern but don't seem to object to tourists drinking in their 'local'.

Jesuit Churches

Consecrated in 1641, as was usual in Jesuit churches, this example was modelled on Gesù II, in Rome, the first church built for that Order. Its architect was a Jesuit brother, Pieter Huyssens, the son of a mason, who designed similar churches in Ghent and Antwerp. During the French Revolution, Sint Walburgakerk became a Temple of Law, but reopened for Catholic worship once more in 1804

brug, the bridge immediately ahead, to Spinolarei. Koningstraat, first left, leads to Sint Walburgakerk, the church that faces Sint Maartensplein.

Sint Walburgakerk

Although Sint Walburgakerk (St Walburga's Church) is only open for half an hour before services or 6–10pm in July, August and September. It is usually possible to view the interior through its glass inner door.

The Baroque interior is remarkable for its sumptuous furnishings and fittings. Worth a visit on its own account is the woden pulpit, carved in 1669 by Artus Quellinus (or Quellin), reputedly the master from whom England's Grinling Gibbons learnt his craft. Quellinus spent a great deal of time sculpting the marble interior of the Royal Palace in Amsterdam and, in consequence, examples of his work are too rarely seen elsewhere. Few pulpits equal Sint Walburga's in dramatic power – a preacher hardly seems to be needed! Particularly striking

is the canopy, which appears to be swept by a powerful wind. Looking up to the pulpit from the floor of the church it is difficult to avoid the searching gaze of the cherubs.

On leaving Sint Walburgakerk, turn left and follow Sint Maartensplein to Boomgardstraat, which leads to Hoogstraat, right.

The **Aarendshuis Hotel**, 18–20 Hoogstraat, rather ambitiously claims that Napoleon and Josephine stayed in one of their rooms in 1811. This is somewhat surprising as Napoleon disposed of Josephine in January 1810, when he arranged for the annulment of their marriage. In addition, although they certainly visited Bruges, it is recorded that the couple slept on that occasion in Sluis (Holland). A three star hotel, there is some Empire-style décor, and six of the rooms have four-poster beds.

Huis de Zeven Toren

On the same side of the road, at number 6, is the **Huis de Zeven Toren**

Places to Visit

Jeruzalemkerk

Peperstraat
Open: 10am–12noon, 2–6pm. (Sat 5pm). Closed on Sun.
Joint admission charge with Kantcentrum.

De Gouden Boom

47 Langestraat
☎ 050 33 06 99
Brewery Visit. Groups (minimum 15 persons) Admission charge includes 1 drink. Only on request.

De Gouden Boom (The Golden Tree) Museum

10 Verbrand Nieuwland
Open: 1 May–30 Sept, Wed to Sun 2–5pm.

Kantcentrum

3a Peperstraat
Open: 10am–12noon, 2–6pm (Sat 5pm). Closed on Sun.
Demonstrations every afternoon. Joint admission charge with Jerzalemkerk.

Guido Gezellemuseum

64 Rolweg
Open: 1 Apr to 30 Sept 9.30am–12.30pm, 1.15–5pm; 1 Oct to 31 Mar 9.30am–12.30pm, 2–5pm. Closed Tue.

Museum Voor Volkskunde

40 Rolweg
Open: 9.30am–5pm daily.

Sint Jorisgilde

59 Stijn Streuvelsstraat
☎ 050 00 54
Open: daily on request.

Engels Klooster

85 Carmersstraat
Open: 2–3.40pm, 4.15–5.15pm. Closed every 1st Sun of the month and church holidays.

Sint Sebastiaansgilde

174 Carmersstraat
Open: Mon, Wed, Fri and Sat 10am–12noon, 2–5pm.

Sint Janshuysmolen

Kruisvest
Open: 1 Apr to 30 Sept 9.30am–12.30pm, 1.15–5pm (depending on wind).

Onze-Lieve-Vrouw ter Potterie

79 Potterierei
Open: 1 Apr to 30 Sept 9.30am–12.30pm, 1.15–5pm. 1 Oct–31 Mar 9.30am–12.30pm, 2–5pm. Closed Tue.

(House of Seven Towers). Only at basement level are there traces of what might be the original stone mansion built for Bonin van den Gapere in 1320. The mansion's distinguishing feature were seven slender towers protruding above the roofline, hence its name, but these were demolished in 1717. King Charles II lodged here during his exile in Bruges during Cromwell's Commonwealth. In return for its hospitality, the English King gave permission for 50 Bruges vessels to fish in English waters.

Diligence, almost opposite, at number 5, serves exceptional food and some of the most economically-priced beer in central Bruges (closed Wednesday and Thursday); and there is a friendly bar at which to sit. Trappist beer is available bottled or draught.

Hoogstraat leads to Markt via Burg.

3. North Bruges

Route 3

Tranquil canals & medieval trading houses

Beginning and ending at Markt, fine weather will help this itinerary, as **Sint Jakobskerk** (St James's Church) is the only building that can be entered. Many of the canal stretches passed will have few visitors, and their relative solitude gives an 'Old Bruges' atmosphere that is unmatched by the more populous waterways.

Sint Amandsstraat

Leading westward from Markt, this is a lively street, most of its cafés and taverns having outdoor terraces. Very soon, the thoroughfare opens up to form a small square, which was created in 1817 when the Sint Amandskapel was demolished. Its place was taken by the huge water pump, a contemporary of the similar pump in Vismarkt. In the Middle Ages, Sint Amandsstraat formed part of the route taken by state processions from Sint Donaas cathedral, in Burg, to the Prinsenhof palace. Sint Amandsstraat ends at the Noordzand-straat/Geldmuntstraat junction, immediately north of which lies Muntplein. The names of both Geldmuntstraat and Muntplein commemorate the building in which coins were minted

*Opposite Page: Augustijnenrei
is regarded as one of the most
picturesque canals in the city*

from around 1300 to 1786; it stood in the adjacent Gheerwijnstraat, but no longer survives.

An equestrian statue of Mary of Burgundy 'Flandria Nostra' stands in Muntplein, the work of Jules Lagae, 1987. Return to Geldmuntstraat, right, first left Prinsenhof.

Prinsenhof

Philip the Good expanded the residence of the counts in Noordzandstraat by adding further courtyards, and the complex, finished in 1429, was named **Prinsenhof**. The previous year, Philip, in search of a third wife, commissioned Jan van Eyck to paint a portrait of the eminently suitable Isabella, daughter of the king of Portugal, to see if he approved of her looks. He did, and the marriage took place in 1430, the

Prinsenhof, now just a Gothic pastiche

Sint Amandsstraat, once the state processional route from Prinsenhof to Burg

wedding feast at Prinsenhof being one of the greatest celebrations in the history of the city. It is said that fourteen ships brought the wedding guests to Bruges, all of them disembarking at the north end of Minnewater.

Order of the Golden Fleece

During the ceremony, Philip founded the Order of the Golden Fleece. Although a lamb's fleece appears to be the source of the Order's name, it has been alleged that the golden hair of Maria Crombrugghe, a Bruges beauty, was the true inspiration. Others see a connection with the Greek Legend of Jason and the Golden Fleece.

Philip's son, Charles the Bold, held an even more splendid wedding feast at Prinsenhof in 1468, following his marriage to Margaret of York, Edward IV's sister. Like his father, the Duke was making a third trip to the altar, but no expense was spared: Burgundian wine flowed from the public water fountains in the streets.

Served at the feast was an immense pastry that enclosed an orchestra. A further surprise for the wedding guests was an artificial whale from within which forty choristers sang.

One of the guests entertained was William Caxton, who would later print *The Recuyall of the History of Troy* at Bruges in 1475, the first book to be printed in the English language. Caxton's task in Bruges at the time was to represent, as governor of their association, English merchants operating throughout the Burgundian Netherlands. Seeing the enormous potential for printing in England, Caxton

returned in 1476 and set up a printing press at Westminster Abbey.

In 1958, it was decided to commemorate the great ceremony every five years in August. Known as the Pageant of the Golden Tree, a procession of two thousand participants dressed in fifteenth century Burgundian costumes parades through the streets. The history of Flanders (Bruges in particular) is depicted in various set pieces, the high spot being the arrival of 'Charles and Margaret' at Bruges.

Those who have visited Onze-Lieve-Vrouwekerk may already have seen the tombs of Charles the Bold and his daughter Mary of Burgundy. Mary gave birth to Philip the Fair at the Prinsenhof in 1479, only to die there three years later following a hunting accident. After her death, the dukedom of Burgundy came to an end, and much of Prinsenhof, by then little used, was sold. From 1622, English Franciscan nuns operated a boarding school for the daughters of wealthy English Catholics in its few remaining buildings. Entirely dimolished by French revolutionaries in 1794, a Boulogne monastery eventually took over the site, building a new Prinsenhof in Neo-Gothic style; some of the ancient fabric was apparently incorporated into the structure. Prinsenhof may not be visited unless attending concerts, exhibitions or conferences, which are occasionally held within.

Undoubtedly, the original Prinsenhof would have incorporated superb Gothic architecture, and it is with a sense of loss that visitors leave the rather unprepossessing square that bears its name.

From the south-west corner of

Prinsenhof, Ontvangerstraat leads northward to Moerstraat, right. After the Gheerwijnstraat/Leeuwstraat crossing Moerstraat opens out to form Sint Jakobsplein, in the centre of which stands Sint Jakobskerk.

Sint Jakobskerk

Sint Jakobskerk (St James's Church) was founded in 1240 as a small chapel. Rich merchants in the locality gave their support, and the building was greatly enlarged in the fifteenth century by the addition of late-Gothic aisles.

Internally, like so many Bruges churches, Sint Jakob has been remodelled in Baroque style. Its patrons included the Duke of Burgundy and the wealthy Portinari, De Gros and Moreel families, with the result that an unusual number of paintings were purchased, almost giving the impression of an art gallery. The most important of these, one of the best known Flemish Primi-

The Legend of St Lucy

Lucy, an extremely charitable Sicilian lady, is depicted giving all her belongings to the poor. She is then accused of being a Christian by her fiancé, who with dismay has seen Lucy dispose of her dowry. Found guilty, she is condemned to work in a brothel, but even with the help of two oxen, the brothel owners are unable to drag Lucy away with them. Although the story is set in pagan Syracuse, the background to the third panel is obviously Bruges – the lantern has not yet been added to the belfry.

tive works, dominates the chapel in the north aisle of the nave: *The Legend of St Lucy* **triptych**, painted in 1480 by an anonymous artist who is known simply as the Master of the Legend of St Lucy. Its caption in Dutch reads *"De legende van de H. Lucia de meester van de Lucia legende 1480"*. (See box below)

The last chapel of the chancel's south aisle is generally regarded as the finest in Bruges. Late-Gothic in style, it was commissioned by Ferry De Gros, Treasurer of the Order of the Golden Fleece, who died in 1544. Forming the top section of a two-tier layout is the joint tomb of De Gros and his first wife, which was probably made in 1521, the year of her death. Their recumbent effigies surmount the tomb. Forming the lower tier and also surmounted by a recumbent effigy is the tomb of the second wife of De Gros, who died in 1530. Above the chapel's altar is a terracotta Virgin and Child medallion in the Renaissance style of the Italian Della Robbia family. Ceramic tiles, contemporary with it, surround the altar.

A splendid brass memorial of 1577, commemorating a Spanish merchant, Francisco de Lapuebla and his wife, embellishes the chapel of the nave's south aisle.

Opposite the north side of the church, from 16 Moerstraat, runs a cobbled lane, approached through double gates that are unlocked during the day. It passes, on the right, a row of almshouses identified as **Vette Vischpoort 1434**. At the end of the narrow lane flows a canal, which is overlooked on its opposite bank by a delightful, flower-bedecked house, the sudden, theatrical appearance of which is quite startling.

Route 3

N
W E
S

Augustijnenbrug
Gouden Handrei
Spaanse Loskaai
Hans Memling Statue
Woensdagmarkt
Augustijnenrei
Kortewinkel
Vlamingbrug
P. Pourbusstr.
Vlamingstraat
Spanjaardstraat
Oosterlingenplein
Genthof
Spiegelrei
Koningbrug
Spinolarei
Engelsstraat
Academiestr.
Jan Van Eyckpl.
Genthof
Vette Vischpoort
St Jakobsplein
Naaldenstraat
A. Willaertstraat
Biskajersplein
Winzak- straat
St Jansstraat
Boterhuis
Kuipersstraat
Vlamingstraat
Kraanpl.
Sint Janspl.
Leeuwstr.
Moerstraat
Gheerwijnstr.
St Jakobsstraat
Eiermarkt
Muntplein
Geldmuntstraat
Prinsenhof
Ontvanger st.
Prinsenhof
St Amandsstraat
Noordzandstraat
Markt
Burg

0 50 100 150 metres
0 50 100 150 yards

KEY

❶ Sint Jakobskerk (St James's Church)
❷ Boterhuis (theatre)
❸ Hof Bladelin (Bladelin Court)
❹ Stadsschouwberg (City Theatre)
❺ Saaihalle (Frietmuseum)
   and Huize ter Beurze
❻ Augustijnenbrug
❼ Tolhuis (Customs House)
❽ Poortersloge (Burgher's Lodge)
❾ Huis de Crone (Choco-Story and
   Lumina Domestica Museum)
▬ Walking route

Sint Jakobsstraat

Return to Sint Jakobsplein and proceed to the east side. Facing the chancel of the church is an ancient example of a red pillar box, apparently still used for letters.

Follow Sint Jakobsstraat from the south-east corner of the square, ad-

jacent to Boterhuis is a range of ten step-gabled houses on the north side, numbers 38-56. Opposite, at number 41, the **Hotel Best Western Navarra** was the mansion of Juan de Peralta, who acted as consul for the Spanish merchants of Navarre in the seventeenth century.

Naaldenstraat, first left, boasts two

Boterhuis

Boterhuis, at number 36, on the north side, was Sint Jakobsstraat, was originally a building used by the dairy trade which operated here from the late sixteenth century until around 1860, when the building became a concert hall; it now accommodates a cafe and a theatre, Theater de Korre. The present Classical facade was constructed in 1830.

Boterhuis (the street) leads eastward from the building and incorporates the small square in which milk and butter (but not eggs) were once sold.

historic buildings. At its south end on the west side stood **Hof van Gistel**, in 1444 the mansion of Antoine de Bourbon, Duke of Vendome, and later the residence of Jean de Matance of Burgos, leader of the important Spanish trading community in Bruges. All that survives is its circular tower, which is best seen from the north end of Naaldenstraat where, at number 19, Hof Bladelin has survived in its entirety.

Hof Bladelin

To enter Hof Bladelin, ring the bell to the right of the doorway, which will then click open. Turn immediately right and ask the attendant (who may not speak English) for the archivist, and wait for her to arrive.

Pieter Bladelin, councillor of Philip the Good and Treasurer of the Order of the Golden Fleece, built the east (entrance) range of the mansion and most of the south range, including its tower, around 1440. Original stone corbels support the vault of the arcade to the house. That to the left of the door depicts a woman with her dog, representing fidelity. The other shows St Alphege of Canterbury holding a bone; he was allegedly martyred in 1012 by drunken Danes who battered him with

animal bones after he had refused to pay a ransom demand).

The range facing the original house was built in 1568, replacing a building that Bladelin apparently kept after he

The Medicis

Piero de Medici, of the Florentine banking family, bought Hof Bladelin in 1466, adding a banking room to the west of the original range – the join can just be seen externally. In 1473, the entrepeneurial Medici representative in Bruges, Tomaso Portinari, resided in the house and was painted by Memling.

Externally, the Medicis left their mark primarily on the arcade fronting the exit. Embedded in its courtyard wall are two Renaissance medallions dating from around 1473 and depicting Piero's son Lorenzo the Magnificent and his wife Clarice Orsini. Within the arcade, corbels are carved with the Medici family emblem of three peacock feathers within a ring. On the bosses of the vault, similar feathers encircle seven red orbs, which signify Piero de Medici. Lorenzo the Magnificent was represented by eight orbs, whilst six orbs signified his grandfather Cosimo – the mathematical logic of a family of bankers!

had disposed of the remainder. Finally, the west range, which overlooks the garden, was added in 1623, thus enclosing the courtyard.

From the delightful rear garden, there are still traces of a second tower that Bladelin had built. Presumably, this was removed by the Medicis when they built their **banking room**. Margaret van Vageriere lived in a house on the south side of Bladelin's estate before her marriage to him.

If convenient, some lucky visitors may be shown the interior of the banking room and Bladelin's salon. The former combines Medici and Burgundian symbols. Repetition of the peacock feathers and orbs already seen will be noted on the beams and corbels. Bugundian mottos *Semper* (always) and *Mon Joi* (my pleasure), their battle-cry, may have been later additions. The fireplace is original.

Bladelin's salon, reached from the banking room, is decorated with paintings executed by a pupil of Raphael in 1521; thses were acquired after the Medicis had left. The arms of Philip the Good and Isabella of Portugal decorate the room. Count Egmont (immortalised by Beethoven in his Overture to Goethe's eponymous play) lived here briefly in the sixteenth century. He was accused of treason by the Duke of Alba and executed in Brussels.

Facing the street, above the entrance to Hof Bladelin, the polychrome sculpture depicts Bladelin kneeling before the Virgin. It is late nineteenth century Neo-Gothic work by our old friend Louis Delacenserie who, no doubt, would have loved to 'improve' the entire house.

Opposite Hof Bladelin, **Hotel Lucca**, originally the trading house of Italian merchants from Lucca, retains a fourteenth-century cellar, now converted to the reception area and a bar. It is believed that bales of silk were once kept there.

Follow Naaldenstraat southward to Sint Jakobsstraat where, immediately opposite, is the **Stedelijk Conservatorium** (City Music School). Towards Markt, **In den Wittenkop** offers good bar food, and opposite, at number 13, **Pietje Pek** specializes in international dishes and an amusing display of menus.

Eiermarkt (Egg Market) is a small but lively square, interrupting Sint Jakobsstraat just before Markt is reached. Most of its buildings now accommodate bars and restaurants, which are extremely popular – and crowded – at weekends.

At number 9, **'t Voske Malpertuus** boasts a restaurant with a medieval monastic cellar. Its speciality is a massive waterzooi fish stew – rich, creamy and served as two helpings. Nearby, Raadskelder is recommended for mussels.

A Baroque water fountain of stone survives in the square.

Herve cheese

Cross to the west side of Eiermarkt. Some will have observed that Belgians rarely eat cheese as part of a three or four course meal, as do their French neighbours; there are therefore few cheese specialist shops to be seen in Bruges.

At number 2 Eiermarkt, however, **De Brugse Kaashoeve** is a rare example in the city. A wide range of French cheeses is stocked, but lovers of real stinkers – the type that, as soon as you put your key in the front door, rushes to greet you, carrying your carpet slippers – will wish to try Herve. Herve, in the form of a square block, is a Belgian cheese that is hardly ever found outside the country. It makes a ripe Camembert seem innocuous and, in deference to those sensitive to powerful odours, should not be purchased until just before returning home. Those travelling by train accompanied by a Herve have a good chance of making the journey in an empty compartment!

Tobacco products are sold at **Tobacco/Giftshop,** 21 Markt at the Markt/Elermarkt junction. Large stocks are held.

Head directly northward from Eiermarkt along Kuipersstraat, passing the city library, **De Biekorf**, left. At the street's north end, **'t Zwart Huis Tavern** at number 23 was built in 1480. Note the brick trefoil Gothic tracery in the niches above its windows.

Facing the tavern, Adriaan Willaertstraat leads to Vlamingstraat. On the right is **Stadsschouwberg**, the city's main theatre, erected in 1869. A statue of **Papageno**, the bird-catcher in Mozart's *The Magic Flute,* stands in front of the building.

In the fifteenth century, this part of Vlamingstraat became the financial centre of Bruges. At that time, the northern sector of the thoroughfare narrowed to little more than an alleyway, and the square created was known as Beursplein (another Beursplein to the south-west of Bruges, has no connection with this one).

Built as the Genoese Trading House in 1399, **Saaihalle** (Serge Hall), number 33 Vlamingstraat, is the only example of a medieval trading house in Bruges to survive, albeit much altered. In addition to importing the usual spices, precious stones and metals, the Genoese specialized in alum from Asia Minor, which was used for fixing leather dyes. It will be noted immediately that the building is faced with a honey-coloured stone rather than the usual brick. This came from a small quarry near Ghent and was extremely expensive, indicative of the great wealth of the Genoese.

The late-Gothic entrance portal is original, including the relief in its tympanum of St George (patron saint of the Genoese) slaying the dragon. The narrow second door and window are twentieth century additions to the rest of the ground floor, which originally comprised a bare wall apart from the entrance. The first floor is little altered. Originally, the upper storey was formed by a false, crenellated wall with two large windows, but this was replaced in 1720 by the present bell gable, a Dutch feature rarely seen in Bruges.

In 1516, the Genoese followed the trend by transferring to Antwerp, and the Serge (Saai) Weavers took over the premises as their trade hall. It now accommodates the **Friet Museum**, everything you could wish to know about chips explained – sampling is included.

Next door, at 35, **Huize ter Beurze** (House of the Bourse), built in 1453, has been faithfully restored to its original appearance by the bank that now owns it. A thirteenth-century inn formerly stood here under the sign of The Three Purses (*beurse* is Dutch for purse). Italian and Spanish merchants conducted their business in the tavern, and trading prices were posted outside, the name *beurse* soon becoming synonymous with stock dealing. The family that had owned the inn since 1276 changed their name to Van der Beurse, and stayed in residence after the present building was constructed, not vacating it until 1483. Meanwhile, their name had been adopted by leading European stock exchanges: *bourse* in France, *borsa* in Italy, *bolsa* in Spain, and *borse* in Germany; England, naturally, preferred to be different, calling their stock dealing centre simply The Exchange.

Beursplein became the Bruges base for Italian merchants; all of them were fierce competitors, and they probably built their trading houses close together so that they could keep an eye on each other. The house of the Venetians stood at the north end of Beursplein until it was demolished for the widening of Vlamingstraat in 1965.

On the Academiestraat corner, the first building on the north side (number 1) occupies the site of the former Florentine trading hall, which was a most impressive building, with slender twin turrets. Now a restaurant, the plaque on its Vlamingstraat side wall quotes Dante's fourteenth century disparaging reference, in *The Divine Comedy*, to the newly constructed Bruges-Wissamt dike. Dante studied in Paris and may have heard about the dike from fellow students, or even visited Bruges himself.

Continuing along Vlamingstraat, **number 51** is a late-Gothic house built for Jacob Cnoop, whose daughter married the painter Gerard

Tolhuis

Mozart's Papageno guards the Stadsschouwberg theatre

An oriel window of number 100 Vlamingstraat

David. The house, with an unusual roofline, was restored in 1996. Also late-Gothic is the building opposite, at **number 82**, with a stone oriel window.

The most splendid oriel window in Bruges, however, is seen by continuing ahead to Vlamingbrug. Right of the bridge at the rear of **number 100 Vlamingstraat**, overlooking Augustijnenrei (the canal), its oriel window demonstrates how richly decorative Flemish brickwork could be. It was commissioned by Herman van Oudvelde, a goldsmith, in 1514. Recently discovered tiny chimneys in the roof of the oriel indicate that the area was used by the goldsmith for smelting.

Before crossing the bridge, some may wish to return to Vlamingstraat and explore Kortewinkel and Pieter Pourbusstraat interconnecting streets that cross it a few paces to the south. Most houses are extremely ancient, with many examples of step gables and even some rare timber façades.

Augustijnenrei & its ancient bridges

The stone-built bridge, **Vlamingbrug**, has low benches that were not seats but platforms on which merchants displayed their wares. Following the north side of the canal Augustijnenrei snakes north-eastward, affording some of the most tranquil scenery in Bruges.

Now supporting a garden on the opposite (south) side of the canal, the curved brick arches are a fragment of the second enclosing city rampart, which was built when the canal was excavated in 1127.

Augustijnenbrug

Augustijnenbrug, the next bridge (built in 1391), also of stone, is supposed to be the city's oldest to survive. It was constructed to provide friars with a short cut from their Augustinian monastery to the city centre. More benches for merchants are similar to those seen on Vlamingburg.

Hotel ter Brughe

Cross Augustijnenbrug to **Spaanse Loskaai**, left, its name announcing that we have entered the former trading quarter of the Spanish merchants.

Jan Van Eyckplein

From Spaanse Loskaai, on the opposite side of the canal can be seen **Hotel ter Brughe**, the most photographed of the city's ancient hotels.

Oosterlingenhuis

A right turn conducts the visitor into the rectangular square known as Oosterlingenplein, and a rapid transition from Spanish to German Bruges has now been made. Oosterlingen literally means Men from the East, as Germans were referred to.

At number 1, adjacent to Hotel Bryghia stands what remains of Oosterlingenhuis, the former Trading House of the Hanseatic League. Their house in Bruges had been founded at a great ceremony attended by an august collection of mayors from four of the League's member cities: Bremen, Cologne, Hamburg and Lubeck. Only the lower sections of the original Oosterlingenhuis, designed for the League by local architect Jan van der Poele in 1478, have survived. The present building has a similar crenellated roof to that illustrated in a seventeenth century print. Above the entrance is the double-headed eagle emblem of the League.

The Germans shipped fur, grain, beer and wine to the city, but unlike their Spanish and British neighbours, never built their own weigh-house. Boycotted economically, the Hanseatic League members were among the first to move to Antwerp.

Ooosterlingenplein merges with **Woensdagmarkt**, the Wednesday market of its name recently transferring from Burg to Markt. The central **statue of Hans Memling** was erected in 1874.

Jan Van Eyckplein & Spanjaardstraat

To the south, Jan Van Eyckplein is one of the most picturesque squares in Bruges. Its **Jan Van Eyck statue** is the late nineteenth-century work of the same sculptor responsible for the slightly earlier figure of Memling just seen.

On the north side of the square at number 2, **Tolhuis** (Customs House) was rebuilt in 1478 for Pieter of Luxembourg, whose gilded coat of arms is carved above the entrance. Through inheritance he acquired the personal right to levy customs duty on goods shipped inland from Bruges; this duty remained in force until the late eighteenth century, and its collectors lived here. Formerly, the canal came right up to the building, and goods were unloaded at Sint Jansbrug, the bridge that faced it but which no longer exists as the canal has been filled in.

Nestling against the west side of Tolhuis is an unusually narrow building, the former **Huis der Lastdragers**, the guildhouse of the Stevedores. Built in 1470, its Flamboyant tracery is typical of late-fifteenth century Brabant Gothic. Note the heads of dockers carved on the corbels.

Spanjaardstraat runs directly northward from the Academiestraat corner of the square. At **number 9**, Ignatius Loyola, founder of the Jesuit Order, stayed during the summers of 1528–30 on vacation from his studies in Paris.

Now a small hospital, **number 16** was built for a Spanish merchant in the sixteenth century. The Renaissance portal is a seventeenth-century addition.

Dated 1616, and also built for a Spanish merchant, Den Noodt Gods (Divine Providence) was the official name of **number 17**, but it became better known as Het Spookhuis (The Haunted House), presumably because ghosts made appearances within; ironically, the Employment Office now occupies the building. It is an astonishingly late example of Gothic work, although the portal is Renaissance – giving the impression of an afterthought.

Return to Jan Van Eyckplein, from the north-east corner of which runs Genthof. On the corner with the square, **number 1** is a castellated late-Gothic house. On the same side, **number 7** possesses a rare Bruges facade of timber.

Spiegelrei

Return to Jan Van Eyckplein and follow Spiegelrei, first left, which curves eastward following the canal.

A vaguely Classical building at **number 13**, now a school, occupies the site of the former house of the English Trading Adventurers. In view of the importance of trade between Bruges and England it is a surprise to learn that the building only stood for ten years.

Koningsbrug

Ahead, cross Koningbrug, right, a hump-backed bridge of stone, built in the fourteenth century, and from where are gained enchanting views of the slender tower of Poortersloge, the delicacy of which is enhanced by morning sunshine.

From the south side of the bridge

turn right and follow Spinolarei. Engelsestraat, first left, which runs southward (no need to enter it) was where the English Merchant Adventurers were permitted to build their own weigh-house, which stood here from the fourteenth to the sixteenth century.

Yet another return is now made to Jan Van Eyckplein, ahead, which is left this time from its south side, via Biskajersplein. This reference to Biscay indicates that we are back once more in the Spanish trading quarter, and at **number 6a** survives the former Den Struys, built in 1510 for Biscay merchants. Along its side appears a splendid Lombard frieze, a feature more usually associated with Romanesque architecture.

Wijnzakstraat runs southward from the square, and on the corner at number 2 is **Huis de Crone**, a fifteenth-century mansion of four bays. Slender chimneys and brick ribs give an apparently greater height to what is already a tall building. Note the delicate trefoil Gothic tracery above the windows. Huis de Crone now accommodates the **Choco-Story** and **Lumina Domestica Museum**. Learn about the development of chocolate and domestic lighting with; 6,500 lamps.

To its south, Wijnzakstraat runs into yet another small square, Sint Jansplein, where there is a four-sided lion's-head **water pump** of stone.

From Sint Jansplein follow Sint Jansstraat westward to **Kraanplein**, a square of no particular visual appeal although Memling incorporated it into his St John altarpiece, now in the Memling Museum. In the Middle Ages, the municipal crane stood in this square, hence its name. Kraanplein leads to Vlamingstraat, left, and thence Markt.

Poortersloge

Poortersloge occupies the west side of Jan Van Eyckplein. Built in the fifteenth century as a traders meeting, it became the headquarters of the Society of the White Bear, promoters of the city's tournaments. A bear, carved on the north side, resides dressed in a festive costume.

The Fine Arts Academy was founded at Poortersloge in 1739, and Academiestraat's name is a reference to it. In 1883, the Academy moved, and the building now accommodates state records.

Places to Visit

Friet Museum
Vlamingstraat 33
☎ 050/34 01 50
www.frietmuseum.be
Open: daily 10am–5pm. Admission charge. Everything about chips explained - sampling included.

Hof Bladelin
19 Naaldenstraat
☎ 050 336434
Courtyard open: 10am–12noon, 2–5pm (4pm 1 Oct–31Mar). Sun and Public Holidays 10.30–12noon. Interior open by appointment.

Lumina Domestica Museum
Wijnzakstraat 2
☎ 050 61 22 37
www.luminadomestica.be
Open: daily 10am–5pm. Admission charge. Domestic lighting museum - primarily lamps.

Choco-Story
Wijnzakstraat 2
www.choco-story.be
Open: daily 10am–5pm. Admission charge. The development of chocolate. Tasting.

4. South-west Bruges

The south-east corner of Simon Stevinplein

Route 4

Shopping streets & the cathedral

This itinerary, like the first, begins at Markt and ends at the station. It should not take long to complete unless a great shopping expedition is planned. Apart from the shops, only the cathedral and two small chapels may be entered; fine weather is certainly an asset. Some may

already have seen the cathedral, which is centrally located, but no detour is involved if it is included, as suggested, on this itinerary.

From Markt, follow Hallestraat, which runs south-eastward skirting the Gothic west range of Halle, built around 1365. Its arcade is basically Renaissance in concept, however, the windows above it remain Gothic. (If wished, access can be gained from the arcade to the central courtyard and thence Markt.)

Right Oude Burg, first left Kartuizerinnenstraat.

Carthusian monastery

The name of Kartuizerinnenstraat refers to the Carthusian monastery that formerly occupied much of it. A Baroque **archway** to the street serves as a memorial to Brugeans killed in both World Wars.

Continue ahead to the former church, built in 1612, which is all that remains of the monastery founded in 1580. In its crypt are the ashes of Dachau concentration camp victims.

Return northward to Oude Burg, where, outside number 4, Irma, a lace shop, a lady sits making lace from 11am to 6pm.

Proceed southward to **Hof van Watervliet**, at number 27, where the entrance block and stairtower survive from the fifteenth-century mansion of Pieter Lanchals, executed by Brugeans in 1488 for supporting Archduke Maximilian's unpopular tax measures. The courtyard may be entered, but it will be seen that the bulk of the mansion, to the south, has been completely rebuilt. It is known that Sir Thomas More and Erasmus visited the house in the sixteenth century, when it was the property of Marcus Laurinus, Dean of Sint Donaas Cathedral and an early humanist sympathiser.

Oude Burg terminates at **Simon Stevinplein**, formerly a market square. The Westfleeshuis (West Meathouse) of the butchers stood here from the thirteenth century, and meat was sold from stalls set up outside the building.

Simon Stevin

The bronze **Simon Stevin Monument**, erected in the square in 1846, commemorates a man of many talents, who was born at Bruges in 1548. Primarily a mathematician, Stevin preceded Galileo by three years in disproving Aristotle's theory that the speed of falling objects was determined by their weight. He also worked on applications of the decimal point, forecasting that all currencies, weights and measurements would eventually be decimalised. Those visitors who are still wedded to imperial measures are requested not to desecrate the monument! Equally important was the system of flooding by sluices, which Stevin, who was also an engineer, devised as a defence measure for use in extreme circumstances. This proved more applicable to Holland than Flanders, and Stevin emigrated to that country, serving as quartermaster in the army of Prince Maurits of Nassau. He died in 1620.

First left Nieuwstraat, where a new addition to the pub scene, at number 9, **Brew Pub de Brugse Bierkaai** brews beers on the premises. Three may be ordered for tasting, from glasses fitted, Ghent style, in a wooden holder. However, will not stand on a flat surface.

Steenstraat

The most fashionable shopping street in Bruges, Steenstraat runs parallel with Oude Burg and passes the north side of Simon Stevinplein. Many of its shops occupy ancient buildings, those of greatest architectural interest lying just east of the square. On the north side, **number 40** was built in 1527 as the Shoemakers guild-house. The guild's emblem, a high-heeled boot, is depicted on the gable. Strips of brickwork accentuate the vertical nature of the building, which stands on a low stone base. There are good examples of delicate Gothic tracery in brickwork above the windows.

Next door, **number 38** is of much later construction, as is apparent from its Baroque appearance. Built in 1765 for the Carpenters Guild, the house would not seem out of place overlooking an Amsterdam canal.

On the opposite side of Steenstraat, M&S (no connection with Marks & Spencer) has taken over **number 25**, a plaque on which is dated *Anno 1620*. This was originally built as the guild-house of the Masons.

A short distance eastward, now part of Kreymborg, **number 19** was formerly the Bakers guildhouse. Its gable is dated 1650.

Return to Simon Stevinplein and turn, first right, into Kemelstraat.

For most, the object of entering Kemelstraat now will be simply to establish the location of its famous tavern **'t Brugs Beertje**, at number 5. This is because it does not open until 4pm (not at all on Wednesdays) but the bar rarely closes before 1am.

't Brugs Beertje

Mine host, Jan de Bruyne, is undoubtedly one of the country's greatest authorities on beer, stocking more than 300 Belgian varieties at all times. He and his expert staff seem to know exactly how each is brewed and from what raw materials. Customers will be informed immediately of the precise alcoholic rating of the ale selected without a check being needed, apparently the barmen have memorised them all.

At 't Brugs Beertje, beer is an extremely serious business, and the hushed tones normally adopted in a church seem to be appropriate. Here can be found the mysterious lambic beers, fermented with the natural yeast only found in 'the Brussels air'. These beers can be flavoured with raspberries or cherries, but they are also available unflavoured (white), when the taste is extremely sour. Lectures on beer take place from time to time in the venerable rear bar, usually on Wednesdays. Enthusiasts are welcome to attend and should check if there is an English language presentation during their stay.

From the 'cathedral of beer' to the cathedral of Bruges is only a few short steps away.

Sint Salvators - kathedraal

Return to Steenstraat, right, and the great tower of Sint Salvatorskathedraal (Cathedral of Our Saviour) will be seen rising ahead from Sint Salvatorskerkhof, the square in which the cathedral stands.

Sint Salvatorskathedraal did not become the cathedral of Bruges until 1834, following Belgian independence. For more than 50 years, since the suppression of Sint Donaaskathedraal by French iconoclasts, there had been no cathedral in the city. The church was probably founded in the ninth century, but its original building was completely

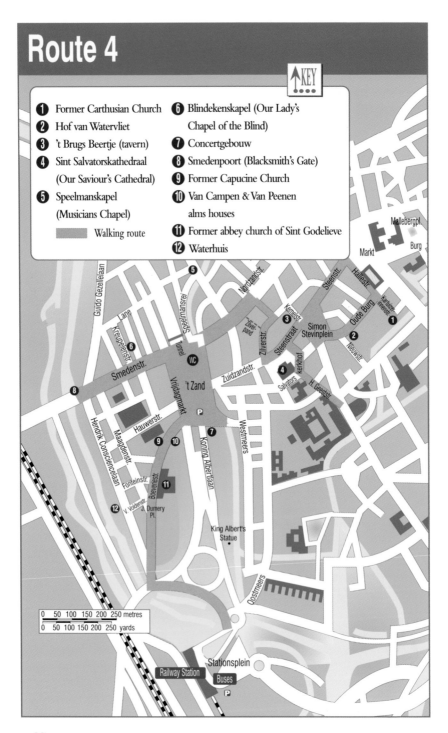

Route 4

KEY

1. Former Carthusian Church
2. Hof van Watervliet
3. 't Brugs Beertje (tavern)
4. Sint Salvatorskathedraal (Our Saviour's Cathedral)
5. Speelmanskapel (Musicians Chapel)

  Walking route

6. Blindekenskapel (Our Lady's Chapel of the Blind)
7. Concertgebouw
8. Smedenpoort (Blacksmith's Gate)
9. Former Capucine Church
10. Van Campen & Van Peenen alms houses
11. Former abbey church of Sint Godelieve
12. Waterhuis

destroyed by fire. All that survives of the church that replaced it in 1127 is the lower stone section of the tower. Its upper storey was lost in the fire of 1853, and rebuilt from funds donated by the English community in Bruges. Unfortunately, the British architect entrusted with the project, Robert Chantrell, decided to employ a neo-Romanesque style, resulting in an unsatisfactory pastiche that had more in common with Norman than Flemish churches. It has been rebuilt more sympathetically in recent years.

The chancel and transepts were rebuilt in the mid-thirteenth century, and most of this work has survived; the present nave, however, was not completed until the early fifteenth century, and Jan van de Poele added chapels to the chancel's ambulatory in 1480.

Interior

Soaring brick vaults and an arcaded triforium at upper level, all with pointed arches, are unifying features of the entirely Flemish Gothic interior. In immediate contrast, on the west wall of the nave is the dynamic organ loft figure of the Almighty, a Baroque masterpiece by Artus Quellin who carved it in 1682.

It may be recalled that the guildhouse of the Shoemakers has been seen in Steenstraat, identified by its high-heeled boot emblem. The same boot can be seen again in the east chapel of the cathedral's north transept, which was built for the Shoemakers Guild in 1372. Here, there are two boots (gilded and surmounted by a crown), one on either side of the Baroque altar of 1667.

The Chancel

Of greatest interest, in the cathedral is the chancel, where the Knights of the Order of the Golden Fleece attended a Chapter in 1478. Maximilian of Austria officiated, and Edward IV of England attended. The misericords of the stalls have been carved in honour of the Order. Above the stalls are the coats of arms of the knights who attended the Chapter. Edward IV's is the first from the left on the north side. The tapestries above the stalls were donated in the eighteenth century.

A series of fifteenth-century late-Gothic chapels punctuates the ambulatory around the chancel. Still a mystery is the possessor of the monogram inscribed immediately right of the date 1513 that appears on the screen to the first chapel on the north side.

The Cathedral Museum

Entered from the west wall of the south transept is the cathedral's **Museum**, which includes treasures inherited from the old cathedral. To assist with dates, remember that *eeuw* is Dutch for century; *relik-wieschrijn* means reliquary.

The museum is accommodated in a nineteenth-century cloister and the adjoining chapterhouse. Exceptional objects to look out for, include: six huge medieval brasses from Sint Donaas; a Renaissance painting of the Virgin flanked by St Eloi and St Luke, by Lanceloot Blondeel, 1545; the silver reliquary of St Eloi, made by Jan Crabbe in 1612; the shrine of St Donaas; and a copy of a lost portrait of Charles V

(Keizer Karel), 1520, by Van Orley.

Heilige Geeststraat

After leaving the cathedral, proceed to the south side of its chancel and follow Heilige Geeststraat (Holy Ghost Street) that runs south-eastward from Sint Salvatorskerkhof. Immediately seen are two ancient buildings facing each other. **Hotel de Castillon,** right, at number 1, commemorates the fifteenth Bishop of Bruges who lived here in 1743. At that time, the name of the house was Huyse 't Pauwkin (House of the Little Peacock), the peacock being a symbol of faith. Now a pension, **Geestelijk Hof,** opposite, at number 2, was formerly the residence of a regional representative known as the Official of Tournai.

The **Bishop's Palace** has been located since 1834 at number 4 Heilige Geeststraat, the former Hof van Pittem. A monumental Baroque entrance leads to a large courtyard facing the Classical mansion built in 1740. It is only open to those on official business.

Return to the cathedral's chancel and follow Salvatorskerkhof anti-clockwise to Steenstraat, left, first right Zilverstraat.

Zilverstraat

There are two buildings in Zilverstraat of particular interest. **Cafedraal,** at number 38, behind its walled garden displays a gable of 1468. It was built for Jean Vasquez, who was the Spanish-born secretary to Isabella of Portugal, and accompanied her to Bruges when she married Philip the Good in 1430.

Proceed through **Zilverpand,** left.

Though the most ambitious covered shopping mall in Bruges, comprises fifty outlets grouped around a court-yard, and linking the north side of Zilverstraat with Noordzandstraat, left. Continue ahead to 't Zand, then turn immediately right along Speelmansrei, which follows the canal. The waterway is unusually narrow and leafy at this point, offering one of the most tranquil stretches in Bruges, which is surprising, considering its proximity to the busy 't Zand. Overlooking the bridge on the Beenhouwerstraat corner is the tiny **Speelmanskapel** (Musicians Chapel), now an art gallery.

Return to 't Zand via Speelman-srei once more. (The parallel street is dreary.)

Speelmanskapel

The Guild of Musicians, which founded the chapel in 1421, acquired the exclusive right for its members to perform at official functions in the city – rather in the manner of a medieval 'Equity'. Large Gothic windows and a brass chandelier are the only features suggesting that the building had been a chapel.

't Zand

In the thirteenth century, the horse and cattle market of Bruges was held in 't Zand; the square now accommodates the general Saturday market, which had been located in Markt until 1983.

The first Bruges railway station opened at 't Zand in 1877, and trains continued to run through the square until after World War II, when the station was relocated to the south and

Tijl Uilenspiegel

Tijl was a legendary figure, according to Belgians a Flemish hero who fought for independence. Under the name of Til Eulenspiegel, however, he is claimed by Germans to be no more than a fourteenth-century prankster, hailing from Schleswig Holstein. Internationally, Tijl Uilenspiegel is better known under his German name, due to Richard Strauss's composition of 1894 dedicated to him.

the railway line diverted. It then became possible to extend 't Zand and lay out gardens on either side to the south; an underground car park (Centrum) for 1225 vehicles was excavated at the same time. Bars and restaurants with summer terraces line the east side of 't Zand, and are as popular with Brugeans as with tourists.

A splendid **fountain**, the finest in Bruges, was erected in 't Zand in 1986, and is the work of Stefaan Depuydt and Livia Canestraro. It is embellished by four sets of allegorical figures as follows: bathing women represent the Flemish cities of Bruges, Antwerp, Ghent and Kortrijk; a horizontal, rather abstract form is meant to suggest the flat polders of the Flemish countryside (below this, on a plaque, are reproduced lines from Dante's Divine Comedy – a repetition of the Vlamingstraat quotation); fishermen are a reference to the industry of Belgium's North Sea, Zeebrugge in particular; cyclists depict youth, and hope for the future. From the top of the fountain, peering in the direction of Damme (once the harbour of Bruges), is Tijl Uilenspiegel (see below).

Smedenstraat

Smedenstraat runs westward from the north-west corner of 't Zand. It is a continuation of Noordzandstraat, and, like that street, a popular shopping thoroughfare – particularly good for food. Follow Kreupelenstraat, fourth right, to the small chapel at number 8. Approached from the alleyway beside the chapel, the **Blindekenskapel** (Our Lady's Chapel of the Blind) is entered from its side door. Happily, the building always seems to be open during the day.

The chapel, probably founded in the fifteenth century, was rebuilt in 1652 and a new, canopied pulpit made for it. Opposite this pulpit, in a silver niche, stands a wooden, part-gilded *Virgin and Child* statue. Below this, the sixteenth-century *Calvary* relief was presented by Francis van Busleiden, Dean of St Donaas.

Suspended from a beam is a model of the three-master merchant ship, *St Michael*, which miraculously docked at Bruges loaded with grain during the famine of 1588 – immediately after prayers to end the famine had been said in this chapel, so it is claimed.

Return to Smedenstraat, right, and continue ahead to **Smedenspoort**, the gateway spanning the road. Built of stone in 1368 but remodelled in 1615, Smedenspoort is contemporary with **Ezelpoort**, the next gate in the ramparts to the north. The bell was rung as a warning whenever the gate was about to be opened or closed. A small bronze skull set in the gate on the Smedenstraat side is a reminder of the Brugean traitor who was executed in 1688 for attempting to open the gate for the besieging army of Louis XIV.

Return to the west side of 't Zand which is still known as Vrijdagmarkt (the Friday Market, which was closed in 1939), and proceed southward.

At the south end of 't Zand stands the **Concertgebouw** music centre, created for the 2002 Cultural Capital of Europe celebrations.

The Bruges Tourist Office now operates from here.

Follow Boeveriestraat, which leads from the south-west corner of 't Zand.

Due to its peripheral situation, **Boeveriestraat**, one of the most historic Bruges thoroughfares, is neglected by the majority of visitors. Many of its buildings are almshouses, identified by their date and owner's name. Even numbers are on the west side. The **Hotel Sofitel**, at number 4, incorporates the façade of the former Capucine Convent, including its chapel.

Opposite, at number 5, the **Van Campen almshouse** of 1436 is linked by a similar building to another important range, the **Van Peenen almshouse** of 1629, which occupies 9–19. Entered through a brick archway to its forecourt, **number 18** on the opposite side of the road is the former monastery of the Capucine friars.

Former Abbey of Sint Godelieve

On the west side, facing Fonteinstraat, is the former Abbey of Sint Godelieve. In a niche above the entrance to the abbey church, which was

The fountain in 't Zand

Boeveriestraat

built in 1623, is a bust of St Godelieve. Strangled and then, just to make sure, thrown into a well by her husband Bertholf van Gistel, Godelieve was canonized in 1084. The original abbey, dedicated to her in the town of Gistel, came under threat from Protestants in 1578 and was abandoned by the nuns, who walked the 21km (13 miles) to Bruges, where they settled the follow-

Procession of the Promise

Following the Battle of the Pevelenberg in 1304, the Flemish gave thanks to the Virgin Mary for their victory over the French by promising to build an almshouse for blind, destitute citizens of Bruges. This event is commemorated every year on the morning of 15 August by the Procession of the Promise, in which a votive candle weighing 13.5kg (30lbs) is paraded through the streets from the Blindekens chapel to Onze-Lieve-Vrouw ter Potterie in north-east Bruges – quite a weight for such a distance.

Former abbey church of Sint Godelieve

ing year. The abbey, sold at the French Revolution in 1796 was regained by the nuns four years later.

From the entrance, it is usually possible to view the interior of the church. At its consecration in 1623, *The Coronation of the Virgin* painting was donated by Monseigneur Dionysius Christophon. His patron saint, St Dyonysius, more usually referred to as St Denis, is depicted on the right.

Just south of the abbey, on the opposite side, Maagdenstraat joins Boeveriestraat on its west side where a small square, Joris Dumeryplein, is formed. Here, protected by great planks of oak is the **Dumery Bell**, named to commemorate the Dumery family, which cast it in their foundry nearby. The bell was brought here from Markt, where it had been rung in the Belfry to warn citizens whenever a major fire broke out in the city.

Van Voldenstraat, a short street, leads westward from Joris Dumeryplein to Hendrik Consciencelaan, which borders part of the open green belt surrounding most of the city. A footpath leads to the **Waterhuis**, built in the fifteenth century as Boevierevest, a pumping station for the city's water supply; horses powered a chain pump to draw water from the canal. Return to Boeverie-straat and continue southward.

Damme

Lying just 7km (4 miles) to the north of Bruges, Damme can be reached from the city by bus or boat. It is a delightful, unspoilt Flemish village, founded in the twelfth century to provide the outer harbour of Bruges. Damme's prosperity ended with the silting upon the Zwin estuary.

Although classed as a village, Damme has its own Gothic church (once with a spire) a town hall, a market square and a medieval hospital. As Damme is approached, either by road or canal, the high tower of Onze-Lieve-Vrouwekerk is the first building seen. Beneath the porch of its tower is buried Jacob van Maerlant, regarded as the father of Flemish poetry, and a Damme resident during the second half of the thirteenth century. Overlooking Marktplein is the Town Hall (Stadhuis), a late-Gothic building, decorated at upper level with carvings representing the counts of Flanders. Standing in the square is a statue of Van Maerlant.

The Tourist Office is located in the Town Hall. Opposite, a 13th century house, Damme's oldest Uilenspiegel Museum, a tribute to the legendary hero said to have been born in Damme.

Charles the Bold married for the third time in 1468, his bride being Margaret of York, sister of England's King Edward IV. The civil wedding took place in the manor house of Damme magistrate Eustaas Wyt, and the building has survived. Also of interest in Damme is the ancient St John's hospital and the old windmill.

city north of the Alps. However, two hundred years later, this had halved to 30,000, wars, sickness and religious strife having taken their toll. Additionally, like Bruges, Ghent was affected by the silting up of the Zwin estuary, although it was never hit quite so badly, due to the Schelde river, which still provided access (slow) to the North Sea. Excavation of new canals was soon to revive Ghent's shipping industry, and early in the nineteenth century the mechanisation of Ghent's cotton industry, achieved by smuggling innovative machinery from England, led to its revival.

Fortunately, unlike London and Paris, prosperity did not lead to the destruction of Ghent's historic centre, where the buildings, while certainly on a larger scale than those of Bruges, still proudly exhibit the splendours of Flemish architecture. Perhaps no other northern European city offers such an

West front of St Baafskathedraal Cathedral

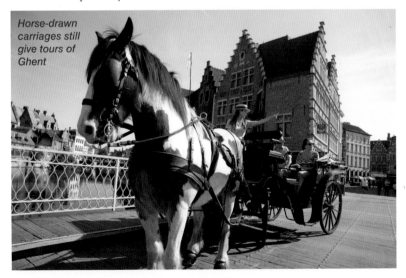

Horse-drawn carriages still give tours of Ghent

intense concentration of attractions, which makes it possible to explore its highlights in just a day (although two days are preferable).

Most tourists visiting Ghent from other Belgian city centres will find it preferable to use the country's excellent train services, particularly as cars are not allowed in the city centre. However, underground car parks are centrally located and reasonably priced. Trains arrive at Gent Sint Pieter's railway station, from where tram 1 departs for Korenmarkt. The first location on the proposed itinerary is Geeraard de Duivelstein, to the east, a ten minute walk away or take tram 4 from Korenmarkt. A return to the station by public transport will naturally be in reverse.

Geeraard de Duivelsteen

(Fortess of Geeraard de Duivel) Not open. The fortress was built of Tournai limestone in 1245 for Geeraard Vilain, a wealthy knight, but only when deputising for the Count of Flanders in his absence did Geeraard occupy the house. He was probably known as Duivel (the devil) due to his grim appearance: great height, dark skin and a long black beard. Much restoration of the fortress has taken place, but Romanesque detailing survives, albeit remodelled.

The north-west wing, in matching style, was added in 1904 to house state archives. In the square facing it, an allegorical bronze of 1913 depicts the seated painters Hugo and Jan van Eyck receiving plaudits. Further west, in Sint Baafsplein, rises the oldest of Ghent's 'three great towers'.

St Baafskathedraal Cathedral

In spite of its uplifting Gothic exterior, Sint Baaf's Cathedral is visited primarily by tourists intent on adoring the 'Adoration of the Lamb of God' altarpiece, a world-renowned polyptich (many panelled) painted by Jan and Hugo van Eyck in the fifteenth century.

A small chapel on this site, dedicated to St John the Baptist in 942, was enlarged and rebuilt several times. However, except for part of its crypt, the present building dates from the reconstruction of the chancel (1300 – 1350) in Schelde early-Gothic style. Not until 1533, did rebuilding of the nave and transepts begin in the more flamboyant Brabant late-Gothic style. Monks from Sint Baaf's Abbey transferred to Sint John's in 1540, which then became monastic and received its present name. The city had never had a cathedral but in 1561, Ghent became a bishopric and Sint Baaf's was elevated to cathedral status.

The tower and west front, 1462 – 1534, were linked to the new nave when it was at last completed in 1559. Originally, the tower had an elegant spire, but this was destroyed by lightning in 1602 and never replaced. On entering, most visitors will immediately turn left and proceed to the former baptistery, now a strongroom, which shelters the renowned Van Eyck altarpiece.

Lamb of God Altar-piece

Brilliant, yet harmonious, colours, realistic detailing and a sense of depth makes it hard to believe that the paintings are almost six hundred years old; a leaflet provided identifies the subject of each panel. Depicted in the lower central panel is the Lamb of God (Mystic Lamb) standing on a sacrificial stone altar, an allegory of Christ's sacrifice on the cross. Flanking this, the first panel, which depicts the Just Judges, is a modern reproduction of the Van Eyck work which together with another panel, was stolen from the cathedral, in 1934, and never recovered.

In the late eighteenth century, it was feared that, in spite of their modestly placed hands, the complete nudity of Adam and Eve in the first and last panels of the upper tier would offend the prudish Emperor Joseph II of Austria during his proposed visit. They were therefore temporarily replaced by clothed versions, but in the event, the Emperor never came.

Proceed to the rear of the altarpiece. Originally, the paintings seen on the reverse side came into view only when the altarpiece was folded. Below the central Annunciation scene, the tier's end panels portray, respectively, Joos Vijd, the donor, and his wife. The John the Baptist panel, next to Vijd, was also stolen in 1934, but returned by the thief as proof that he possessed the other, for which an extortionate ransom was demanded but refused. Many believe that the panel survives hidden within the cathedral.

Joos Vijd, a wealthy magistrate, commissioned the work for his private chapel from Hugo van Eyck, the elder brother of the more famous Jan, in 1424. Having planned the content of the twenty-four panels, Hugo died in 1426, and the project was completed by Jan, who signed and dated the work 1432 and is probably responsible for most that can

be seen. No other painting by Hugo has been identified with any certainty.

The first of the north aisle chapels was the original baptistery, and, by tradition, Charles V was baptised in its font in 1500; the font's cover is nineteenth century work. On the west wall of the north transept, the painting of Sint Baaf's acceptance by a monastic fraternity is by Rubens, 1624: his distraught daughter now faces penury as her once wealthy father is obliged to dispose of all his possessions. By tradition, the central figure in a red cloak is Rubens himself.

Opposite, steps descend to the crypt. At this, the west end, the earliest features of the cathedral survive in the form of Romanesque piers dating from 1150, although they were painted in the fifteenth century. This crypt, one of the largest in a European church, has been extended eastward in stages, as explained by a chart on the west wall. At the east end, in the central chapel, another famous treasure of Sint Baaf's is a Calvary tryptich altarpiece by a fifteenth century painter whose identity is unknown, even though Justus van Gant is optimistically credited.

Return to the north transept, from where it can be appreciated that the vault of the chancel is slightly higher than that of the nave. The nave's outstanding furnishing is its Redemption pulpit of 1745, carved in Rococo style by Laurent Delvaux.

In the sanctuary, the Baroque high altar is early eighteenth century work; the tomb chest in front of it, to the left, commemorates Anton Triest, Bishop of Ghent 1621–57, and a generous benefactor of the city. This is the work of Jerome Duquesnoy, who sculpted

Ghent

0   140   280 metres
0 50 100 150 200 250 yards

Meelstraat

Bachtenwalle

Sint Antoniuskaai

Academiestraat

Tempelhof

Sluizeken

Kaatspel Plein

Sanderswaal

Patershol

Oud Begijnhof

Prinsenhof

㉙

Burgstraat

㉔ ㉕

Kranlei

㉝ **Vrijdagmarkt**

㉚

㉒ ㉗

㉖ ㉑

㉛

Bij Sint Jacobs ㉜

㉓ ㉒ ㉕

㉗ ㉖ ㉑

㉒ ㉐ ㉑

Korn Inutraat   Luxemburgstraat

⑰ ⑲ ⑱

Vlas Markt

Oude Schaap Markt

Hoogstraat

⑮

St. Michielsbrug

⑯

⑤

Koren Markt   Klein Turkije

⑭

Sint Michielsbrug

⑩ ⑧ ⑥ ⑦   ④

Bover Markt

③

⑬

⑨

Cataloniestraat

Sint Baafss Plein

Kapittel

②

Schouwvegersstraat

⑫

⑪

Wilderossstraat

Jonkvrouw Mattest

Zwartzustersstraat

Wellingstraat

Brandstraat

Pussemierstraat

Hoornstraat

De Kuip

Voldersstraat

Geraard De Duivelhof

①

Posteernstraat

Maagdstraat

Annonciaden Straat

Zandpoortstraat

Zonne Straat

Schouwburg Straat

Early morning sun illuminates Sint Michelsbrug – before sightseers arrive

the original Mannekin Pis fountain in Brussels.

On the south side of the cathedral, a reproduction of the Lamb of God altarpiece occupies the Vijd chapel, for which the original was made; it stood here until 1986 (apart from occasional sojourns abroad at the command of foreign invaders).

Ghent

Café culture on the street in Vridagmarkt

Beside the first pier right of the cathedral's exit are the painted, clothed figures of Adam and Eve that temporarily replaced the originals in the Lamb of God altarpiece.

Exit from the cathedral, right. From Sint Baaf's east end, Biezelstraat curves northward.

Number 1, Biezelstraat, dated 1901, is a rare city centre example of the Art Nouveau style.

Ahead, at the first bend left, **Achter Sikkel** is the rear (achter) courtyard of the Grote (large) Sikkel, a mansion built for the wealthy Van der Sikkel family in the fourteenth century; its façade is seen later. The red brick tower survives from that building, but the remainder was mostly reconstructed in the fifteenth and sixteenth centuries. In the northwest corner, the chapel was erected over the family's well. A Renaissance-style octagon crowns the white stone tower. The arcade, right, served as a monastic sanctuary during Ghent's religious turmoil, but the arcade, opposite, was added in the last century for the sake of symmetry.

Continue to the end of the street and cross to the north side of Nederpolde, facing number 2, **Kleine** (small) **Sikkel**, on the Biezelstraat corner. This, the Van der Sikkels' first house, was built early in the thirteenth century and retains its Romanesque cellar. Carved in the tympanum of a ground floor window is a sickle, the family's punning coat of arms. Below this window, a recess indicates the original position of the front door. The castellated roofline of the house was created during twentieth century restoration.

When built on the opposite Biezel-straat corner, in the fourteenth century, the close proximity of **Grote Sikkel**, 64 Hoogpoort (its rear courtyard has just been seen) gave the Van der Sikkel family additional space without having to relocate. The step gable was added in 1481. Internally, the building was connected with the adjacent De Moor house in 1901, and together they now accommodate a Music Academy.

Follow Hoogpoort westward. First left Botermarkt. Built in 1477, number 2 **Sint Jorishof**, the step-gabled corner house, is surmounted by a figure of Saint George (Sint Joris), signifying that it had been the guildhouse of the crossbowman's Guild of Saint George. Its grounds incorporated an extensive archery practise range. Many historic receptions have been held within the building, and until recently the Sint Jorishof claimed to be the oldest hotel in Europe. Its future use is uncertain. Opposite, Stadhuis occupies the west side of Botermarkt.

Stadhuis (City Hall)

Admission when convenient or by prior group arrangement. Designed in the flamboyant Gothic style of Brabant, this was planned to be Europe's tallest city hall. Construction along Hoogspoort of its **Huis van de Keure**, where legal and accountancy matters would be handled, began in 1482, but money ran out in 1535 and work on the project was halted. Not until 1595 could it be resumed, but sixty years had passed and Renaissance, not Gothic, was the architectural style now favoured. Consequently, the **Huis van Ghedele** (for civil arbitration officers), which stretches the length of Botermarkt, is a rather severe example of the Italian Renaissance, apart from Flemish touches to its dormer windows. Each of the fifty-six niches on the Gothic facade was meant to be occupied by a statue, but none had been installed when building stopped; the nineteen examples now in place are modern. The Treaty of Pacification was proclaimed to the public in 1576 from the first floor balcony overlooking Botermarkt. Continue ahead to the Belfry.

Belfry (Belfort)

Open daily 10am – 5pm, 1 March – 30 October. Admission charge. This is the highest of Ghent's medieval towers, at 91m (298ft) and 8m taller than its Bruges rival. Work began in 1314, but only a timber superstructure, which would need frequent replacement, could be afforded. Eventually, in 1913, the present white stone structure was built – six hundred years later than planned. A gilded copper dragon, replaced whenever necessary, has surmounted the belfry since 1377, symbolising Ghent's commercial strength.

The belfry's set of great bells is housed on the third floor, the largest of them, Klokke Roeland, cast in 1948, is rung to announce the start of the Ghent Festival in July. Its predecessors were sounded to announce the approach of invaders, the execution of notorious criminals and the arrival of state visitors. Two floors accommodate an exhibition; a combination of steps and a lift lead to the summit, with its magnificent views of the city below.

Entered from Sint Baafsplein, a basement tourist office will make hotel bookings. Open 9.30–6.30 in summer (closes 4.30 in winter), it is planned that this will transfer to the old Fish Market in 2010.

Lakenhalle (Cloth Hall)

Adjacent to the Belfry is **Lakenhalle** (Cloth Hall). Not open. This hall, where merchants sampled, bought and sold woollen cloth, was begun in 1425, but when it was just four bays short of its intended length, work was halted due to a decline in the cloth trade. Not until 1913 were the last four bays added – although it is hard to tell the difference, so well do they match the earliest section of the building. Immediately west of Lakenhalle, the square's name, Emile Braunplein, commemorates Emile Braun, the late-nineteenth century burgomaster who was chiefly responsible for demolishing houses in order to create Sint Baafsplein, as well as this square, thereby opening up views of the Cathedral, Belfry and Sint Niklaas Church. Proceed to the square's south-west corner.

Displayed here since 1950 is the great **Triumphant bell**, cast in 1660 for the Belfry, which cracked in 1914 following an attempt at electrification. It was never called Klokke Roeland, the name of the first – and the present – great bells.

Opposite, number 1 Cataloniestraat was built in the sixteenth century as the **Masons' Guildhall**, but its façade was completely renewed a few years ago. The gable has been embellished with six delicate weathervanes in the form of gods, devils and men, each cavorting exuberantly on a pinnacle; unexpected but delightful levity in this area of civic grandeur. Continue westward to the east end of Sint Niklaas Church.

Sint Niklaas (Nicholas) provided

Medieval goings-on at Gravensteen

The cathedral illuminated at night

Ghent's watchtower until the Belfry was built. An eleventh century Romanesque building on the site burnt down and was replaced 1200 – 1250 by this Schelde Gothic church, which has changed little externally throughout centuries of restoration and extension. An exception will be observed at the east end (seen first) where an ambulatory with radiating chapels, in Brabant Gothic style, was added in the sixteenth century. As was usual in Ghent, religious strife destroyed all Gothic fixtures and fittings, but in some compensation, their Baroque replacements have increased the lightness of the interior, which had always been blessed with unusually deep windows; particularly worthy of note is the exuberant high altar. Due to its proximity to the Corn Market and the port, wealthy merchants and guild members had private chapels in Sint Niklaas, resulting in the wealth of Flemish art displayed. Particularly moving is the painting of the

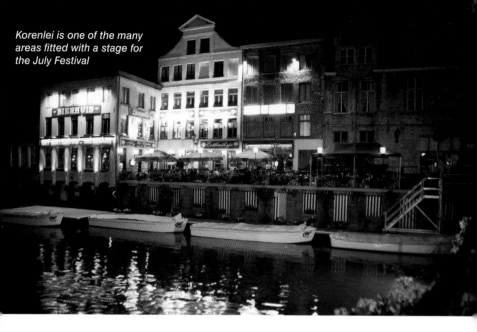

Korenlei is one of the many areas fitted with a stage for the July Festival

Van Minjau family, which (including its 31 children) was to be exterminated in the plague of 1526. Exit to Korenmarkt, left, which leads to Veldstraat.

Unless looking for clothes – preferably black in colour during autumn and winter – visitors will find little of interest in Veldstraat. However, half way down, two Louis XV mansions (hôtels)

face each other. On the east side, built in 1768, number 55, **Hôtel d'Hane-Steenhuyse** is where Louis XVIII and his followers stayed for almost one hundred days in 1815, fleeing Napoleon, who had just escaped from Elba. Opposite, number 82, **Hôtel Arnold van der Haeghen**, was built two years earlier. Wellington lodged here just

Stadhuis: a famous mix of styles – Gothic to the north, Renaisance to the south, left

Ghent's three great towers stand on parade

prior to Waterloo in 1815 in order to discuss the situation with the French king-in-exile.

Return to the north end of Veldstraat, turn left and continue ahead to Sint Michielsbrug (Saint Michael's Bridge). An ancient flat bridge, its predecessor, was rebuilt in 1913 and given an arch to aid navigation. Views northward over the Leie river provide some of Europe's finest townscapes, and the outstanding houses of its famous quays, Korenlei (west side) and Graslei (east side) are explored shortly. Graslei, the finer of the two, is best seen (and photographed) when late afternoon sunshine strikes its buildings. Equally splendid, from the western approach to the bridge, are the views of Ghent's 'three towers' which from this point appear to stand in line, one behind the other, like guardsmen on parade. Here again, the best photographic results are obtained in late afternoon, when the sun strikes the towers.

Sint Michielskerk

Immediately south of the bridge is **Sint Michielskerk** (Saint Michael's Church). Building commenced in 1440, but the tower did not reach its present height until 1672; as its flat roof and stumpiness suggest, a much taller structure had been planned, but funds ran out. Only usually open for services, the most important work of art within is the north transept's Crucifixion scene of 1630 by Van Dyck. Return to the bridge and descend the steps to Korenlei, proceeding northward.

Korenlei

From the eleventh to the nineteenth centuries, trading vessels sailed to and from Ghent's ancient port, prosaically called Tusschen Brughen (Between the Bridges), mooring at its quays. For convenience, merchants and shippers built their imposing guildhouses and warehouses directly overlooking the river, and many of their facades (but not their interiors) have fortunately survived, albeit restored and frequently altered. Number 24, the former **Guildhouse of Beer Export Workers**, a Renaissance building of 1664, is supported by the ground floor of its thirteenth century predecessor.

The ancient facades of numbers 10-9, which now front the new **Ghent Marriott Hotel**, have been preserved, but behind them all is completely modern. The sixteenth century façade of number 9, now **Marriott's Corn House Restaurant**, originally fronted an inn, which brewed beer. Its name, De Zwaene (The Swan), a symbol for beer, is commemorated by the swan emblem on its wall. Apparently, the services of young ladies were also offered within: by tradition, an incognito Emperor Charles V paid a visit in the sixteenth century.

Number 7, formerly the **Guildhouse of the Unfree Boatmen** (Onvrije Schippers) is now a restaurant. It was built in 1663, the year in which the law banning its guild members from operating in Ghent's port was rescinded. Prior to this, the Unfree Boatmen had to transfer their cargoes to the Free Boatmen at the approaches to Ghent. The Rococo façade, its gable surmounted by a gilded caravel weathervane, dates from 1739.

Seen here, across the river in Graslei, six adjoining houses provide the quintessential example of Flemish domestic architecture. To inspect each house closely, cross Grasbrug, the first bridge ahead, descend to Graslei and proceed southward.

Graslei

Very few Graslei houses are identified by their original functions or even numbered; however, most are now restaurants, so if confused just ask a waiter. Fortunately, number 8 is quite easily located by its profusion of Gothic pinnacles. Built in the sixteenth century as the **Mason's Guildhouse**, an additional storey was added in 1912 and the whole completely refaced in Brabant Gothic Revival style. An angel coyly reveals the earlier name of the house: Der Enghel (the Angel).

Number 9 was first built in 1435 as the **Corn Measurers Guildhouse**, but most that survives dates from 1540, the year in which the guild relocated to number 12 a few doors away.

Number 10 **Staple House**, built c.1130, is the oldest step-gabled house in the Low Countries, and miraculously, some Romanesque features have survived. Its original basement is now the entrance floor, evidence of the rise in ground level. Until 1734, corn was stored within in lieu of paying customs duty, but a fire in 1896 destroyed the interior completely.

Number 11, **Tollhouse**, believed to be the smallest house in Ghent, was built in 1698 by filling in a narrow alleyway. Here lived the custom officers appointed to collect taxes on merchandise shipped to Ghent's port. To prevent excessive corruption, the officers were replaced annually.

Number 12-13, **Corenmetershuys** (Corn Measurers House). Needing more space, it was to two existing buildings on this site that the Guild of Corn Measurers transferred from number 9 Graslei in 1540. Remodelling to unite the properties must have taken place soon after, but the present red brick façade dates from 1698.

The gold sandstone façade of number 14, formerly the **Guildhouse of the Free Boatmen**, is generally regarded as Ghent's finest. The Free Boatmen purchased the house from the Millers Guild in 1530, and within four years had completely refaced it in the present transitional Brabant Gothic / Renaissance style. Above the door is an intricately carved caravel. Above this, the arms of Ghent, Flanders and Burgundy are followed by those of Charles V and his motto *plus oultre* (even more).

Return to the north end of Graslei, from where boat trips depart and return. These last around 45 minutes (vessels are covered in bad weather) but not all boats will offer English commentaries – check before booking. Apart from the usual pleasures of river trips, the most important location seen is the Rabot, as it is some distance from the city centre.

Located at what is now the terminal point of the Lievre Canal (excavated in 1251), the Rabot, built in 1491, is a fortified lock, virtually all that remains of Ghent's medieval defences. Its stepped façade and rounded turrets with their conical roofs are very romantic, but the effect is marred by inappropriately located tower blocks of flats hovering menacingly in the background – reminiscent of 1960s British iconoclasm at its worst.

Two of Graslei's great houses: Staple House and Corenmatershuys with the tiny Tolhouse inserted between them

On returning to Graslei, proceed northward to Pensmarkt, a popular spot for al fresco snacks in fine weather.

Stretching along the river bank, the **Groot Vleeshuis** (Great Butchers Hall) was built in 1404 to comply with legislation that meat had to be sold from a roofed building. At its Pensmarkt end, however, offal (pens) could be bought by the poor from lean-to structures set up externally against the hall's east wall. The hall is open to the public, but no meat has been sold here since 1884. Most of the interior is now a low-price

From Sint Michielsbrug the Leie River bisects Korenlei and Graslei, Gravensteen's turrets forming a backdrop

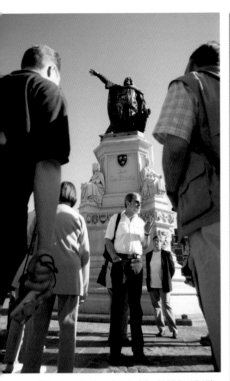

The Jacob Van Artevelde (1290–1345) monument in Vridagmarkt commerates a close friend of England's Edward III

restaurant, with a separate section for selling local produce, some of which, e.g. honey, mustard, ham, can be tasted before purchase. The original timber roof survives.

Fronting the meat hall is **Groentenmarkt** (Vegetable Market), one of Ghent's minor medieval horror spots. It was judged the ideal location for pillories, due to the plentiful supply of rotten fruit and vegetables from the market stalls, with which cowardly sadists could pelt hapless victims.

In the corner, number 5, **'t Galgenhuyseken** (Little Gibbet house), attached to the north end of the Meat Hall, is Ghent's smallest and most atmospheric tavern. Built in 1783, its name suggests that hangings took place nearby, but this might be just gallows humour, referring to the strength of the beer sold within. When crowded, and in this tavern three is a crowd, eight more can be coped with upstairs and more outside. Behind the tavern, attached to the wall of the Meat Hall, are hooks to which those condemned to be pilloried were fastened.

Ferdinand Tierentyn, at number 3, has made gourmet mustard for many years. Apparently, the skins of Tierentyn's mustard seeds are not removed before manufacture; the result has a slightly thinner texture and burns the mouth less than Dijon mustard.

Return towards the river and follow the waterside path, right, which is still called, surprisingly, Groentenmarkt. Ghent's best known genever (gin) house, **Dreupelkot**, at number 12, does not open until 4pm, but should be visited if possible. Ask for an oude (old) genever; a smooth, smoky 12 year old Belegenjenefer is recommended. Do not dream of ordering a Dutch gin; all gins sold here have been patriotically distilled in Belgium. Exit right.

Groentenmarkt is closed by **Het Waterhuis,** at number 19. As the name suggests, customers can sit overlooking the water while drinking from a wide choice of Ghent beers: try a fairly strong Gandavan Dry Hopping, low in fizz but high in flavour, as proper lager should be, i.e. unlike UK brews. The three Groentenmarkt taverns, virtually on top of each other, are unmatched in charm by either Bruges or Brussels – a great mini pub crawl. Exit and return westward. First right, cross Vleeshuisbrug to Sint Veerleplein.

Sint Veerleplein, due to its proximity to the grim Castle of the Counts, which overlooks it, was undoubtedly Ghent's horror centre between the fifteenth and eighteenth centuries. All imaginable, and some unimaginable, punishments were publicly inflicted here on unfortunates sentenced by the castle's terrifying law courts. Genuine criminals, but also those found guilty of 'heresy' and 'witchcraft', were tortured, disembowelled, burned to death, hanged, beheaded, boiled in oil etc. in this relatively small square, to the delight of baying onlookers. Apparently, women were not burned, as, being the inferior sex, they were judged unworthy of municipal expenditure on firewood – so they were drowned instead. The central pillar supporting a lion, erected in 1913, marks the location of the burning stake, and later the guillotine.

Still occupying the square's south-west corner, the **Vismarkt** (Fish Market) buildings of 1680 were extended in 1872. A massive Baroque gateway of 1689 is guarded by an unusually svelte Neptune threatening to poke intruders with his trident. Below, reclining male and female figures are allegories of Ghent's two rivers, the Schelde and the Leie respectively. Fish has not been sold here for many years, but after a long period of inactivity, work is in progress adapting the complex to become Ghent's Tourist Information Centre – due to open in 2010. From the square's north-west corner, **Onthoofdingsbrug** (Decapitation Bridge) crosses the Lieve Canal. By tradition, criminals were beheaded on the bridge itself at dawn, following a night in the cell built into the structure below it.

Some believe, however, that the name refers to executions in the adjacent Sint Veerleplein. From the bridge can be seen a cream-painted house, the last timber frontage to survive in Ghent. Once there were over 500 similar examples, but a destructive fire in 1490 resulted in a judicial insistence on brickwork. Return to Sint Veerleplein and approach Gravensteen from its north-east corner.

Gravensteen (Castle of the Counts)

Open daily 9am–6pm. Admission charge. The complex is primarily a nineteenth century reconstruction of the castle built in 1180 by Philip of Alsace, Count of Flanders.

This had replaced an eleventh century castle of stone, which itself had been preceded by a ninth century timber fortification. In the mid-fourteenth century, the Counts of Flanders acquired another large palace nearby, which they restored and refurbished luxuriously, soon transferring their residence to it from Gravensteen. The new palace, named Prinsenhof, like the Bruges Prinsenhof, has virtually disappeared, only its donkere poort (dark gate) surviving.

The fortress later accommodated a mint, law courts, torture chambers and prison cells. In the eighteenth century, the castle was sold for industrial use, which included two cotton mills. By 1887, much of Gravensteen was in ruins, and demolition seemed probable. Fortunately, the municipality, aided by the state, purchased the complex and restoration was completed by 1913. This work, supplemented by more recent reparations, has resulted in the present romantic, if not entirely authentic, Gravensteen.

Prisoners awaited sentence in the upper room of the Gatehouse, which linked with a small torture chamber, but really serious torturing took place in the keep's cellar. In some instances, presumably when the crowd might riot in sympathy with the condemned, an execution would take place beneath the archway of the gatehouse in an area demarcated by two bars. Spectators could thereby observe that the sentence had been carried out without being able to do much about it.

However inaccurate the reconstruction of the castle might be, it is immediately apparent that, as elsewhere in Ghent, Romanesque origins, when applicable, have been respected, and thick walls, small apertures and round-headed arches are ubiquitous. It is still obvious that the ground and first floor walls of the eleventh century keep had been retained as a base for the present structure. Attached to the keep, the step-gabled building originally housed the count's private quarters.

Clear signs indicate the route to follow and the areas as they are seen. Interior decoration is minimal, as in the contemporary Tower of London, and most is, quite rightly, left to the imagination. Of interest to the ghoulish are instruments of torture, a replica guillotine with an original blade (last used in Ghent in 1861) and an oubliette – a tiny, black, underground cell (now illuminated) – in which prisoners were thrown and literally forgotten.

Exit right from Gravensteen and return to the east end of Sint Veerle-plein, where it meets Kleine Vismarkt (Small Fishmarket). Number 2, beside the bridge (Vleeshuisbrug), an elegant Louis XV style house, now a restaurant, was built as the **Wine Merchants Guildhouse** in 1755. Barrels of wine were hoisted by crane from the Leie to its cellars, which have survived from the earlier structure. The crane that gave Kraanlei its name stood conveniently adjacent to the building.

Behind Kraanlei, the Patershol district has become very fashionable, and some of Ghent's finest restaurants can be found in its narrow, winding streets. **Bij den Wijzen**, 42 Herstogstraat, is Patershol's oldest, and the first Ghent restaurant to be awarded a Michelin star. Its waterzooi is reputedly the city's finest. Adjacent, at 6 Plotersgracht, **Vier Tafel**, specialises in unusual meats – crocodile, kangaroo, etc. Hard to believe that even after the Second World War had ended, Patershol remained the dangerous, vice centre of Ghent, parts of which the police declined to enter. Continue eastward following the Kraanlei riverside to number 65.

Museum voor Volkskunde (Folklore)

Open Tuesday–Sunday, 10am to 6pm, April to October and November to March. Admission charge. This museum spreads over eighteen small houses built around a central square; a tranquil scene that masks a violent origin.

Two wealthy but long-feuding Ghent families, Rijm and Alyn, belonged to separate trade guilds that were also in dispute, and in 1354, during Mass at Sint John's Church, brothers Simoen and

Vridag Markt is the major venue for the Ghent Festival

Goswijn Rijm stabbed to death two of the Alyn brothers Hendryk and Seger. The killers fled, but were sentenced to death in their absence. Surprisingly, both received pardons eight years later, with the stipulation that they had to finance a hospice. This was built in 1363 to care for poor, elderly women, and named the Hospice of the Alyn Children (the murdered brothers were actually young men). In 1962, after extensive remodelling, the complex opened as a folklore museum, presenting day-to-day artefacts from around 1900 in appropriate room

Gravensteen, city centre castle

Ghent's three great towers beyond Sint Michielsbrug

Ghent's slender Post Office tower

settings. Although, as would be expected, these nostalgic 'time capsules' will mean more to Belgian than to foreign visitors, few will leave without a slight moistness in their eyes.

Exit and continue to Kraanlei, where, at numbers 79 and 81, built on the corner with Rodekoningstraat in 1669, are two of Ghent's most splendid Flemish Baroque facades. Number 79, known as **The Seven Works of Mercy**, a reference to their depiction on the façade panels, has been for many years the famous Temmerman's, where home-made confectionery in many forms is sold. Children from eight to eighty will find it irresistible.

Adjoining, and even more flamboyant, number 81 is known either as **The Flautist** or **The Flying Deer**, from its façade's terracotta subjects. Also depicted are the five senses and, on the gable, Faith, Hope and Charity. Cross Zuigelbrug, right, and continue ahead to Vrijdagmarkt.

Vrijdagmarkt (Friday Market)

A general market has been held on this, Ghent's largest square, since 1199, and it has also long been the venue for state receptions and public rejoicing. In February 1500, the entire square was flooded so that ice skaters could celebrate the birth of the future Holy Roman Emperor Charles V at Ghent's Prinsenhof Palace.

Royal Connections

Charles was the nephew of Catherine of Aragon, and, on sacking Rome in 1527, he instructed Pope Clement VII not to approve Henry VIII's divorce from his aunt. Without Charles's intervention, England might still be Catholic. Also born in the city in 1340 was John of Gaunt (Ghent), fourth son of Edward III, uncle of Richard II, and father of his usurper Henry IV

As might be expected, notorious criminals, whose public execution would attract greater crowds than Sint Veerleplein could accommodate, were usually beheaded here: the last such barbarity took place in 1822. Almost as bloody were the fights between opposing trade guild members, which regularly occurred in Vrijdagmarkt, often ending in deaths.

Formerly, a statue of the unpopular Charles V stood in the centre of the square, but in 1863 the present monument was erected to the 'Sage of Ghent', Jacob van Artevelde (1290-1345). Artevelde's close friendship with England's Edward III did much to preserve Flemish neutrality during the Hundred Years War, thereby protecting Ghent's all-important textile trade. However, not all agreed with Artevelde's policies and, returning home from a meeting on the night of 17 July 1345, he was murdered.

With the prominent exception of the bulky, early twentieth century, **Ons Huis** (Our House), headquarters of left-wing unions, the square retains many of its ancient buildings. Of greatest interest to most is **Het Toreken** (Little Tower), number 31, in the south corner, built in 1483, which was the Tanners Guildhouse until 1540. Its white turret, crowned with a mermaid weathervane, still shows the influence of the Schelde-Gothic style. Some original carving survives in the building's former guildhall, which may be visited during exhibitions. Adjacent, the neck-gabled number 25, c.1770, was built as the **Linen Makers' Guildhouse**.

On the south-west side of the square, **Numbers 47** and **49** are delightfully Baroque. From the latter, in the eighteenth and nineteenth centuries, dignitaries addressed the crowds, a revival of the medieval tradition set by the counts of Flanders, who made important announcements to Ghent citizens in the square.

Visitors will find that most Vrijdagmarkt restaurants cater for those on a budget. Nevertheless, steaks are inevitably tender and tasty, chips, as always in Belgium, are superb, and a carafe of wine won't break the bank.

To the east, the Romanesque tower of **Sint Jacob** (Saint James), a short distance away, overlooks the square. This is all that remains from the twelfth century building, the rest is Gothic or Gothic Revival work carried out between the thirteenth and nineteenth centuries. Within, as is usual in Ghent, the original Gothic features have been replaced by Renaissance.

By tradition, the commencement of **Gentse Feesten** (the Popular Culture Festival) is marked by enthusiastic youngsters, who gather to celebrate in the square outside the church. Every year, for ten days, from the last Saturday preceding 21 July, concerts are given in virtually all Ghent's city centre squares, which are then closed to traffic and become open-air concert halls, each with a stage. All types of music are represented and admission is always **free**.

Extending northward from the west corner of Vrijdagmarkt, the name of the small **Grootkanonplein** (Great Cannon Square) refers to its mid-fifteenth century occupant named Dulle Griet (Foolish Lass) or Mad Meg. Around 5m long and weighing 16,400kg, this medieval weapon of mass destruction was brought to Ghent in 1578 to repulse the Spanish. However, a 340kg stone cannonball was fired from it and managed to travel a distance of – one metre – irreparably cracking the gun's barrel. In spite of this spectacular failure, Dulle Griet has retained the affection of Ghent's citizens over five centuries, reminiscent of the way in which the British admire a plucky loser. From this square, Langemunt followed by Kortemunt lead southward in a straight line to Korenmarkt, the tram departure point. Tram 1, on route to Sint Pieter's Station, passes close to (ask the driver in advance) **Stedlijk Museum voor Actuele Kunst** (MSK) in Citadelpark. Admission charge. Closed Monday. The permanent collection comprises works from the fourteenth century to the present. Star attractions include paintings by Hieronymus Bosch, Breughel the Younger, Kokoschka and Magritte. Local boy James Ensor's 'Old Lady with Masks' will delight many.

Bruges

ACCOMMODATION

Accommodation of all kinds can be difficult to obtain in Bruges outside the winter months, particularly in August when important festivals are held. Tourism Flanders will provide an illustrated list of hotels, bed and breakfast establishments and camping sites on request, and advance booking is advisable. Hotels are categorised from one to four stars, but all rooms, whatever their grade will have a private toilet and shower. Bruges is a compact city, and the advantage of a reasonably central location is obvious. Room tariffs are not dissimilar from British equivalents. Many will be attracted by the hotels that have been adapted from century-old houses, some of which retain period features and are furnished with antiques.

For those arriving at Bruges without pre-booking, a free hotel reservation service is provided at the railway station and the central tourist office in 't Zand.

Recommended centrally-located hotels

A map showing the locations of recommended accommodation in Bruges can be found on page 3. The number next to each entry refers to its map location and the A is in reference to Accommodation.

For dialling codes from abroad see Telephones on page 123.

Four Star

Brughe (ter) **A2**
2, Oost Gistelhof
☎ 050 340324
Fax 050 338873

Bryghia **A3**
4, Oosterlingenplein
☎ 050 338 59
Fax 050 341430
This is a small, exquisitely furnished period building, which was originally connected with the Hanseatic League's Bruges headquarters.

Crowne Plaza **A19**
10, Burg
☎ 050 345834
Fax 050 345615
An ultra modern hotel overlooking the Town Hall. Its basement incorporates fragments of the old cathedral. Facilities include a swimming pool and a sauna.

Best Western Navarra **A10**
41, St Jakobsstraat
☎ 050 340561
Fax 050 336790
As its name suggests, the building was formerly the Trading House of the Navarre merchants.

Orangerie (De) **A38**
10, Kartuizerinnenstraat
☎ 050 341649
Fax 050 333016
The Orangerie is one of the most centrally located hotels in the city and, although small, is very highly regarded for its standard of service and beautifully proportioned rooms.

Relais Oud Huis Amsterdam **A4**
3, Spiegelrei
☎ 050 341810
Fax 050 338891
Overlooks the tranquil Spiegelrei canal and the medieval Poortersloge.

Three Star

Adornes A5

26, Sint Annarei

☎ 050 341336

Fax 050 342085

Occupying a step-gabled sixteenth-century building, the Adornes has rooms with views over the adjacent canal.

Duc de Bourgogne A24

12, Huidenvettersplein

☎ 050 332038

Fax 050 344037

Another centrally located canal-side hotel with outstanding views.

Grand Hotel Oude Burg A37

5, Oude Burg

☎ 050 445111

Fax 050 445100

A large, modern hotel, the Grand is located immediately behind the Belfry.

Ibis Brugge Centrum A47

65a, Katelljnestraat

☎ 050 337575

Fax 050 336419

All 128 rooms have bath and shower. The Ibis is located in one of the city's major shopping streets – a little to the south of centre.

Two Star

Cordoeanier A16

18, Cordoeanierstraat

☎ 050 339051

Fax 050 346111

This is the most conveniently located of all the two-star hotels in Bruges.

Europ A1

18, Augustijnenrei

☎ 050 337975

Fax 050 345266

Augustijnenrei is generally regarded as the prettiest of all Bruges canals.

Imperial A11

24, Dweersstraat

☎ 050 339014

Fax 050 344306

Although a small hotel, the Imperial's rooms are well-equipped. Its building is step-gabled.

Lucca A40

30, Naaldenstraat

☎ 050 342067

Fax 050 333464

Fourteenth-century rooms survive in this friendly, family-run hotel, once the trading house of the Italian merchants from Lucca.

Salvators A36

7, Sint Salvatorskerkhof

☎ 050 331921

Fax 050 339464

Accommodated in another period building. Hotel Salvators lies directly behind the cathedral.

Voermanshuys ('t) A16

14, Oude Burg

☎ 050 341396,

Fax 050 342390

Within a short walk of all major sights of Bruges.

One Star

Koffieboontje ('t) A28
4, Hallestraat
☎ 050 338027
Fax 050 343904
Small, but its outstanding central position, rare in this hotel grade, and well-fitted rooms will suit many.

Putje ('t) A29
31, 't Zand
☎ 050 332847
Fax 050 341423
Also small, the rooms of 't Putje are most comfortable. Slightly to the west of the city centre.

'H' Grade

Central A15
30, Markt
☎ 050 331805
Fax 050 346878
Reasonably priced, no hotel in Bruges could be more central than the Central, facing south over the city's main square.

Patritius A18
11, Riddersstraat
☎ 050 338454
Fax 050 339634
Very centrally located, rooms are fresh and well appointed.

Guest Houses

Mrs Deloof A9
14, Gheerwijnnstraat
☎/Fax 050 340544

Mr and Mrs Gheeraert A17
9, Riddersstraat
☎ 050 335627
Fax 050 345 01

Mrs Nyssen A8
50, Moerstraat
☎ 050 343171
Fax 050 331783

Mrs de Vriese A21
40, Predikherenstraat
☎ 050 334224

Electricity
Voltage in Belgium is 220AC. Twin-point sockets are universal, but as these do not quite accept British twin-point plugs a continental adaptor is necessary. A single adaptor that converts British three-point and two-point plugs to continental two-point sockets is recommended. For US visitors a two-pin continental adaptor is recommended.

Emergencies
For all types of emergency ring 100 (no prefix or payment required).

Festivals & Events
Exit, published monthly, lists each month's attractions in the city; it can be obtained free in advance from Belgium Tourist Offices or on arrival in Bruges.

May

Ascension Day (mid May)

Procession of the Holy Blood. An ancient Bruges tradition, the procession through the streets to the Holy Blood Basilica in Burg celebrates the arrival of the relic in the city.

July

Flanders Festival of Early Music (July/August)

15 August: Blindekens Procession. Established 700 years, the procession leaves the Blindekens Chapel and continues to Our Lady of the Potterie.

August

Festival of the Canals (second half of August)

Held every three years, performances at various canal-side locations take place over six evenings. Tableaux are illuminated, and performances begin at 9pm, each being repeated at 15 minute intervals. It takes three hours to reach all of them on foot.

Pageant of the Golden Tree

Held every five years since 1958, this pageant takes place on two consecutive evenings. Around 100 groups take part in both 2-hour long performances. Primarily, the pageant commemorates the marriage of Charles the Bold and Margaret of York in 1468. High spots are the arrival of the groom in Bruges and a 'medieval' tournament held in Markt.

Getting to Bruges

Ferries

P&O Ferries

(☎ 08716 645 645) operate a nightly Hull/Zeebrugge ferry (14 hours).

Trans Europe Ferries

(☎ 01843 595 522) Operates ferries from Ramsgate to Ostend (14½. hours)

Direct Ferries / Norfolkline

(☎ 08718 900 900) Operate ferries from Ramsgate to Ostend (4½ hours) and daily from Rosyth to Zeebrugge.

P&O Ferries

(☎ 0870 600 0600) Operates Dover/Calais ferries (75 minutes).

Car

The autoroute E40 Calais-Bruges was completed in 1997, and few motorists will wish to use any other route through the rather uninspiring Pas de Calais countryside. Journey time will be around one hour, and there are no frontier formalities at the France/Belgium border. From Ostend it will take around 15 minutes to Bruges by car or local train). Although Zeebrugge is only 20 minutes away by car or train allow longer if you are catching the ferry.

Tourist Coach

Many UK tour operators include Bruges on their coach schedules, although accommodation for their clients is frequently arranged at the nearby beach resorts of Ostend or Knokke. From south-east England regular day-trips are made and it is possible, on occasions, for longer stays to be made, returning on another 'day trip'. Despite paying twice, this is almost certainly the cheapest way to make the journey.

Train

Eurostar trains, for foot-passengers, via the Channel Tunnel (Res ☎ 0870 518 6186), make the journey to Brussels Midi from St Pancras International in one hour fifty-one minutes, from Ebbsfleet in one hour fourty minutes, and from Ashford International in one hour thirty minutes. From Brussels Midi, frequent inter-city trains take fifty minutes to reach Bruges. Alternatively, there are trains from Lille to Bruges and Brussels.

Confusingly, station signs at Brussels read both Bruxelles Midi (French) and Brussel Zuid (Dutch) but it is the same station, i.e. the Eurostar terminal. After passport control, a descent must be made for other rail destinations. Trains to Bruges, which usually seem to depart from platform 16, are indicated via Gent (Ghent) to their terminal at Oostende (Ostend) or Blankenberg. Ensure that the train taken is an IC (inter city) otherwise the journey time will be much longer. Eurostar tickets to Brussels Midi may also be used onward to Brussels Central (one stop) without extra charge.

Apart from the standard fare, which is aimed at the business traveller, a wide range of tariffs is available. Always enquire for the best deal.

Tickets may be purchased or collected on arrival at St Pancras, Ashford or Ebbsfleet, international stations but they can be posted in advance, time permitting. Travel agents also provide Eurostar tickets but may charge a fee below a certain booking value.

'Le Shuttle' trains, for passengers with motor vehicles, (Res ☎ 0870 353 535) also use the tunnel. Drivers to the Folkestone terminal should turn off the M25 at Junction 11A just outside Folkestone. The journey to Coquilles, near Calais, takes thirty-five minutes.

Air

Many UK international airports operate services to Brussels, the most convenient airport for Bruges (flying time 30 minutes from Heathrow or Gatwick). Trains from Brussels Airport reach Brussels Central Station in 30 minutes, and from here the same train services as from Brussels Midi take 50 minutes to Bruges. Flights to Antwerp are not recommended for those continuing directly to Bruges as a change of train must be made at Ghent. When comparing journey times between air and other forms of transport bear in mind that passengers must now arrive at airports at least two hours before flight departures due to security requirements.

Health

For emergency medical service in Bruges at weekends ☎ 050 813899; during weekday nights ☎ 050 516376. For an ambulance dial 102.

Internet Information

Email: toerism@brugge.be or Website: www.brugge.be

Measurements

Metric measurements operate in Belgium. For overseas visitors it may help to remember that 1 kilometre equals approximately ²/₃ of a mile, 1 kilogram weighs just over 2lb, 100 grammes is approximately ¼ lb and 1 litre is slightly less than two pints.

Money

In 2002 Belgium adopted the euro at a fixed rate of 40.3399 Belgian francs to 1 euro. Existing Belgian currency ceased to be legal tender after February 2002. Euro notes are issued in 500, 200, 100, 50, 20, 10 and 5 denominations. There are 100 euro cents to €1 and coins are in 1, 10, 50 and €1 denominations. As Great Britain is not a member of the Eurozone the exchange rate of the pound sterling and the euro is variable. The US and Canadian dollar rates to the euro are also, of course, variable.

Opening Times – Museums And Churches

Specific opening times are given for locations throughout the book. Every church in Bruges is closed from 12 noon–2pm.

A combined entry ticket at a reduced rate for leading museums is available from the Tourist Office or at any of the museums included in the scheme. Most museums in both Bruges and Ghent now close on Mondays, but remain open throughout the year.

Passports

A current full passport is required from all those entering Belgium, whether they are from an EU member country or not.

Postage

Postage stamps may be purchased from many small shops, including book shops and tobacconists in addition to Post Offices. Post Offices are open Monday to Friday 9am–12noon and 2–5pm. Pillar boxes are red.

Public Toilets

Virtually all public toilets in Bruges are manned by women, who will insist on a fixed payment being made in advance by both sexes. Many toilets (men's at least) do not have as many doors as seem necessary.

Public Holidays

On public holidays, virtually all shops and banks are closed. These are: **New Year's Day**, **Easter Monday**, **1 May**, **Ascension Day** (mid May), **All Saints Day** (1 November) **Armistice Day** (11 November), **Christmas Day**. **Flemish National Holiday**, 11 July, and **Independence Day**, 21 July, are also holidays for banks and public offices, but shops remain open.

Recommended centrally-located Bruges Restaurants

A map showing recommended restaurants can be found on page 3. Each is given an R prefix (Restaurant) followed by a map location number. The following restaurants are recommended, but should not be regarded as an exclusive selection. Price categories are per person and include three courses but not drinks.

RESTAURANTS – Over 75 euros

Duc de Bourgogne R24
12, Huidenvettersplein
☎ 050 332038
This top class hotel serves high quality French cuisine in its canal-side restaurant.

Kapittel ('t) R19
Crowne Plaza Hotel, 10, Burg
☎ 050 345834
The hotel's restaurant specializes in gastronomic weekends. Closed Sundays, Saturday lunch, Wednesday dinner.

Karmeliet (De) R20
19, Langestraat
☎ 050 338259
Classical French cuisine, fish dishes in particular. Awarded 3 Michelin stars.

Snippe (De) R43
53, Nieuwe Gentweg
☎ 050 337070
The tops in quality and price. French is served in the most delightful dining room. Fish dishes specialities. Closed Sunday, Monday lunch.

Swaene (Die) R22
1, Steenhouwersdijk
☎ 050 342798
Gourmets should not miss this classic French restaurant.

Patrick Devos' 'De Zilveren Pauw' R33
41, Zilverstraat
☎ 050 335566
Patrick Devos, a young restaurateur of the year, prepares innovative dishes, with many fish specialities. An eclectic wine list. Closed Sunday and Monday.

RESTAURANTS – 50–70 euros

Bhavani R34
5, Simon Stevinplein
☎ 050 339025
At the time of writing, this is one of only two Indian restaurants in Bruges. The other is Indian Tandoori, in Oude Gentweg ☎ 050 345826.

Braamberg (Den) R39
11, Pandreitje
☎ 050 337370
Delicious lamb and fish specialities are the highlights of Den Braamburg's classic cuisine. Closed Sunday and Thursday.

Celebrations Entertainment R35

86 Vlamingstraat
☎ 050 347572
Located in a former Gothic revival church, this 'medieval' entertainment, includes a four-course banquet, unlimited wine and beer. Particularly fun for children. Hawks soar, hounds yelp, a fire-eater eats fire, and the 15th century wedding of Charles the Bold and England's Margaret of York is re-enacted. Kitsch but the enthusiasm charms. Friday and Saturday evening throughout the season.

Kasteel Minnewater R48

4, Minnewaterpark
☎ 050 344254
Set in a nineteenth-century Gothic fantasy castle, this fish speciality restaurant overlooks the romantic lake. A vast summer terrace. Closed Thursday.

Lotteburg De R41

43, Goezeputstraat
☎ 050 337535
A top class restaurant specializing in fish. Closed Monday and Thursday (unless public holiday).

RESTAURANTS – 35–50 euros

Begijntje ('t) R45

11, Walstraat
☎ 050 330089
This tiny restaurant, with only 20 covers, serves regional dishes and reliably tender steaks. Closed Sunday and Wednesday evenings.

Belle Epoque R32

43, Zuidzandstraat
☎ 050 331872
Regional dishes concentrate on fish dishes.

Central/Sirène d'Or R15

30, Markt
☎ 050 331805
Definitely not a tourist trap in spite

Paspartout (De) R6

1, Jeruzalemstraat 1
☎ 050 346613
Good for large parties, game is served in season. Closed Sunday dinner and Monday.

Spinola R7

1, Spinolarei
☎ 050 451785
Set in a pretty period house, there are several lamb specialities – and a renowned apple tart.

Visscherie (De) R23

8, Vismarkt
☎ 050 330212
As may be expected, fish is the speciality here. A definitive waterzooi is served. Closed Tuesday.

of its Markt location. Central offers a varied menu at reasonable prices, which concentrate on game and seafood.

Oud Brugge R26

33, Kulpersstraat
☎ 050 335402
Particularly good for large parties (karaoke facilities). Meals are served in a vaulted thirteenth-century cellar.

Sint-Joris

29, Markt
☎ 050 333062
This is another Markt restaurant that can be recommended. Excellent fish waterzooi and eels are the specialities. Closed Thursdays.

RESTAURANTS – Below 35 euros

Breidel – De Coninck R25
24, Breidelstraat
☎ 050 332746
Renowned for its huge mussels. Closed Wednesday.

China R31
45, Zuidzandstraat
☎ 050 332154
This Chinese restaurant also serves an acceptable Indonesian rijsttafel – primarily, one supposes, to please visitors from Holland where this dish is popular, even though it is rarely prepared with sufficient chillies.

Due Venezie (Le) R27
2, Kleine Sint-Amandsstraat
☎ 050 332326
Probably the best Italian restaurant in Bruges. Closed Thursdays.

Maximiliaan van Oostenrijk R46
17 Wijngaardplein
☎ 050 334723
Outstandingly good value, although the closest restaurant to the famous Begijnhof. Excellent grills, Flemish stews, fish and waterzooi. Outside tables.

Michelangelo R42
16, O.L.V. Kerkhof Zuid
☎ 050 333893
Seasonal and fish dishes.

Raadskelder R13
21, Eiermarkt
☎ 050 343132
Mussels are rated among the best in Bruges.

Voske Malpertuus (,t) R12
9, Eiermarkt
☎ 050 333038
Superb waterzooi is served in two helpings. One room is a medieval cellar. Closed Thursdays.

Telephones/fax

All telephone booths in Bruges only accept cards only; these can be purchased at similar outlets to postage stamps. From Belgium, the dialling code for the United Kingdom is 0044, then dial the number omitting the initial 0 of the local code. For USA and Canada 001, and Eire 00353. To telephone Bruges from abroad dial 0032, followed by the number, but omitting the initial 0. Within Belgium, now including Bruges itself, the dialling code for Bruges is 050.

Time

Belgium is one hour ahead of UK time throughout the year.

Tipping

The service charge is always included in hotel and restaurant bills, and additional gratuities are not expected. However, for very exceptional service, a small additional amount is welcomed. No tips to taxi drivers, boat excursion commentators or horse-drawn cab drivers are necessary.

Tourist Information

Belgian Tourist Offices

England

Flanders House, 1A Cavendish Square, London, W1G OLD
☎ 0207 307 7739

USA (and Canada)

www.visitflanders.us

Tourism Flanders

IT & UIT 't Zand 3t
3–8000 Bruges
☎ +32 50 444646
email: toerisme@brugges.be
Open daily 10am–6pm.

Bruges Railway Station Office

Open: 1 October to 31 March, Monday to Friday 10am–5.30pm, Saturday 9.30am–5.30pm, 1 April to 30 September, Monday to Saturday 10.30am–6.30pm.

Transport – Local

Bicycle Hire

The flatness of most of Belgium has resulted in the great popularity of cycling. Bruges encourages cycling by permitting bicycles to be ridden in each direction along streets that are one way only to motor vehicles. Some hotels loan tricycles to their clients. Hiring points are as follows: Luggage Department, Railway Station, Stationsplein; 't Koffieboontje, Hallestraat 4; Eric Popelier, Mariastraat 26 (also scooters); De Ketting, Gentpoortstraat 23.

Boats

Popular boat trips to Damme from April to September run from Noorweegse Kaai in north Bruges. To reach the boarding point, take Bus 4 from Markt. Trips along the Bruges canals run daily 1 March to 30 November from 10am–6pm. In December and February they operate only at weekends; there are several boarding points, beginning south of Burg, and each trip lasts 30 minutes.

Buses

Staff at the local bus information kiosk outside the station will advise on which bus route passes a required address in Bruges. If several bus journeys are anticipated, a ten-journey pass (Stadskaart) should be purchased from the kiosk, which reduces the total cost by almost 50 per cent. Single journey tickets may also be purchased at the same kiosk; they must be cancelled on entering the bus. As Bruges is so compact, and its narrow streets can only be viewed sensibly on foot, few bus journeys will be needed within the city apart from returning from the station at the end of the two southbound itineraries suggested in this book. However, it should be borne in mind that most will have to make a trip to the station for their homeward journey via Brussels, and some, in addition, will wish to make several train journeys from Bruges to other parts of Belgium, which will necessitate more bus journeys to the station. In the summer, those who plan to visit Damme, Ostend or Zeebrugge by regional buses, can board them either at Stationplein or 't Zand. In winter, there is very limited public transport to Damme, but Ostend and Zeebrugge can always be reached by regular train services.

Horse-Drawn Carriages
These depart from Markt (Burg on Wednesdays) and proceed to the Begijnhof, where they pause before returning. Up to four people can be accommodated. Services begin at 10.30am and in summer will continue usually until 10.30p.

Motoring
Everywhere on the continent, vehicles drive on the right side of the road, give priority to vehicles approaching from the right, and proceed anti-clockwise at roundabouts. UK motorists in Belgium must, by law, display a GB sticker and keep with them in their car a red triangle for use as a breakdown warning if needed, and a basic first-aid kit. Whilst not a legal requirement, a green card for third party insurance is recommended.
Once having arrived in Bruges, the car should be parked as soon as possible. There are underground car parks at 't Zand, Zilverpand, Pandreitje, Biekorf and the station, all of which charge. The latter provides free bus tickets to the city centre.
Strangers will find driving within the ancient city of Bruges a nightmare, with around 50 ever-changing, one-way streets to be negotiated. For the brave, remember that free parking is permitted in a blue zone, but only for the time indicated, and a parking disc, obtainable from any service station, must always be displayed showing the arrival time. Spaces in blue zones are extremely hard to obtain. Parking meters are expensive and can never be used for more than 3 hours. Between 7pm and 9am, and throughout Sundays and bank holidays, unlimited parking is free in blue zones and at meters.

Police
Hauwerstraat 7, ☎ 050 448844

Taxis
On arrival, many will take a taxi from the station to their hotel – and be astonished by the enormous fare demanded; this is partly because the driver's return to base must be paid for. Belgian tariffs are among the highest in the world – it is most unlikely that the visitor is being cheated. For those to whom the cost of fares is unimportant, there is another rank in Markt, and hotels, of course, will book cabs for their clients, when the charge will be even more horrendous. No taxis are permitted to ply for hire.

Trains

From the only railway station in Bruges, situated at Stationsplein, trains depart for all major destinations in Belgium. There are frequent services to Ostend, Zeebrugge and Ghent, and the journey time to each should not exceed 20 minutes.

It must be said that due to its extreme westerly location, Bruges is not the most convenient base from which to make nationwide tours. Belgium, however, is a small country, and as long as an early start is made, day trips from Bruges are possible to Antwerp, Brussels, Leuven, Ghent, the Ardennes – and even Luxembourg at a push.

Many visitors will have journeyed to Bruges via Brussels, and some may find it more convenient to coincide a Brussels trip with the first or last day of their holiday – thus saving time and money. Left luggage facilities are provided at both Brussels Midi (Zuid) Station (for the Channel Tunnel) and Brussels Central Station, which is more convenient for visiting the city centre – the stations are close to each other and on the same line from Bruges. Bruges trains will stop at the three Brussels stations: Midi, Central and Noord. International trains depart from Brussels Midi only.

It is imperative that Intercity (ic) trains are taken whenever possible, otherwise journeys can become very tedious. Stopping trains are indicated by L. If a great deal of rail travel is envisaged, some may find it convenient to purchase a B-Tourrail ticket, which offers unlimited travel throughout the Belgian rail network for varying numbers of days as required, during a one month period.

Index

Published in the UK by:
Horizon Editions Ltd,
Trading as The Horizon Press
The Oaks, Moor Farm Road West, Ashbourne, DE6 1HD
Tel: (01335) 347349
E-mail: books@thehorizonpress.co.uk

6th Edition
ISBN: 978-1-84306-438-1

Print: Gomer Press Ltd, Llandysul, Wales
Cartography & Design: Michelle Prost

Front Cover: Dusk at Spiegelrei Bridge **Back cover, top:** The Belfry from Rozenhoedkaai **Back cover, middle:** The Provincaal Hof, Markt **Back cover, bottom:** From Sint Michielsbrug the Leie River bisects Korenlei and Graslei, Ghent **Back cover, right:** Belgian Chocolates

Picture Credits

Christopher Turner: 42 bottom, 54, 55 bottom right, 63 bottom, 70, 78 top, 79, 82, 103 bottom two

Lindsey Porter: 11 top, 23, 27 bottom, 30, 31 bottom, 43 top, 50 top, 51 bottom, 55 top, 58 bottom, 62 top left, 62 middle right, 63 right, 71 all, 78 bottom, 83, 90, 91, back cover top

Bruges Tourist Information Office: 27 top, 38, 62 top right, 70, 71 mini pic, 78 top, 79 top, 79 bottom

Ghent Tourist Board (www.visitghent.be): 94, 95 all, 98, 99, 102 all, 103 top, 106 bottom, 107, 110 all, 111 top, back cover bottom

Diamantmuseum: 50; Universal Studios: 15

All images below courtesy of www.shutterstock.com with copyright to:

St Nick: 54, 62 bottom right, Front cover; Jan Kranedonk: 19 mini pic, 31 top; Patrick Hermans: 11 bottom, 6; Rostislavv: 46; Daniel DeSlover: 34; Palis Michael: 14 left; Insuratelu Gabriela Gianina: 19; Andrea Seemann: 26; Tony De Laender: 55 mini pic, 63 right; Skyfish: 42 top; Kkaplin: 18; Regien Paassen: 7 top, 14 top; Marianna Raszkowska: 14 bottom right, 7 mini pic